EMOTIONAL FIRST AID

by

John R. Fishbein, Ph.D

Printed in the United States of America
Library of Congress Catalog Number: 91–077776
Emotional First Aid
Covenant Communications, Inc.
Printed February 1992
ISBN 1–55503–376–8

About the Author

John R. Fishbein received his bachelor's degree in business administration from the University of Southern California, and his Ph.D in individual, marital, and family therapy from Brigham Young University. He has been in private practice in San Jose, California since 1975. He also provides consultations for companies seeking solutions for management and personnel problems. In addition, he conducts on-going training in counseling skills for hundreds of church leaders.

Dr. Fishbein is a clinical member of the California Association of Marital and Family Therapists. He hosted "Turning Points," a weekly radio program that focused on handling personal, family and business challenges. He has always been actively involved in church service, including currently serving in a lay leadership position. He is married to the former Shelly Hatch. They reside in Cupertino, California and are the parents of six children.

Acknowledgments

To the extent this book contains correct principles, I gratefully acknowledge the influence of the Lord, whose guidance I seek daily. I wish to express my love and gratitude to my wife, Shelly, for her helpful suggestions and her unwavering faith in me and to our children, Shane, Shannon, Melissa, Chad, and Kristi for their love and support. I also wish to thank all those who have allowed me the privilege of sharing their personal struggles and successes during their journey in life, many of whose experiences are contained in this book. Finally, I wish to acknowledge the superb help of Darla Hanks Isackson in editing and preparing this manuscript for publication.

Table of Contents

PREFACE

For years I resisted invitations to write a self-help book because I did not believe it would have much lasting value to the reader. Most people read such a book once, then put it on the bookshelf to gather dust. However, my wife, Shelly, suggested I do something along the lines of a first-aid book—an emotional first-aid book—one to which people could refer from time-to-time as needed.

This book is designed to be used the same way you use your medical first-aid book. You refer to it periodically when you have a problem to be solved or when you just want more information about a particular concern. You may turn to it for your own needs or to help a loved one or friend. It is a reference book.

In preparation for writing an emotional first aid book, I made a list of the common problems people brought to me in my private counseling practice. These became the topics I have addressed. This volume contains four of those common concerns: **Communication Difficulties, Depression, Unsatisfactory Intimacy,** and **Anxiety Attacks.**

This book is patterned, to the best of my ability, after the same approach I use in my office. As I wrote, I tried to anticipate and respond to your concerns just as if we were talking face to face. If you and I were personally discussing a problem—concerning yourself or someone else—I would provide you with practical, problem solving principles and specific steps to apply the principles. Your questions would receive immediate and direct answers. We would identify barriers interfering with solving the problem and then come up with steps to remove the barriers.

CENTRAL PRINCIPLES

I find that underlying just about every personal problem is the violation of some basic principle. These principles are like the roots that support and feed a beautiful tree. When the roots are strong and unobstructed, the tree bears good fruit. When the tree is bearing some undesirable fruit, the problem and, therefore, the solution, is usually found in the roots.

Most everyone I see has a generally well developed, healthy root system. Among all the healthy roots, however, there are sometimes one or two roots which are undeveloped or obstructed by some barrier. I approach personal problem solving by identifying the roots that need strengthening and the barriers that need removing. Then, rather than hacking at the branches of a problem, we focus on the root of the problem—understanding and applying correcting principles.

The type of counseling I do could be referred to as principle-centered counseling. I have identified eight principles that are central to solving personal problems. Although these are not intended to represent all principles that apply to solving personal problems, they are the ones I find most useful.

From the first moment I talk with a client, I am looking to see what principles they are effectively or ineffectively utilizing. Once we identify a principle that is not fully understood or effectively being used, I suggest specific steps to better understand and apply that principle. By strengthening the roots (central principles) and removing barriers, you can effectively prevent and solve many personal problems.

Even though you may not be applying a central principle effectively in one area of your life, you may be applying it effectively in another area. For instance, at work or with friends you may clearly distinguish between what you can control versus what you cannot control (Central Principle 4), while with a family member you may inadvertently try to control someone or something that is not within your control.

During a counseling session, as well as in this book, I take an active role in teaching principles and suggesting practical applications. I find when I teach correct principles people naturally tend to govern themselves more effectively. As you increase your understanding and application of correct principles, you will discover exciting possibilities for personal progress.

BARRIERS TO SOLVING PROBLEMS

Another key aspect of the counseling I do pertains to identifying and removing barriers blocking the pathway to success. If, despite your best effort to solve a problem, you are not getting anywhere, there is probably something getting in your way. Unless those barriers are identified and removed, your continued effort is apt to feel like hitting your head against a wall or going in circles. I suggest specific, practical steps to remove these barriers. As barriers are removed, you become free to fully use your own vast resources and potential to solve the problem.

A FINAL WORD

Occasionally in my paractice I make reference to faith in God, each person being a child of God, the value of prayer and scripture study, etc. Likewise, occasional references appear in this book. In my practice, if I am working with someone who is not comfortable with such concepts I immediately cease making references. Although I find these concepts helpful, I have the utmost respect for each person's beliefs and encourage you to consider the information in this book in light of your own experiences and beliefs.

For ease of writing "he" is respectfully used to refer to a person without any specific reference to a man or woman.

Like any first-aid book, this book is not designed to be a substitute for those already involved with, or needing, professional help. Nor is it intended to provide a comprehensive treatment program. It can, however, be used as a valuable resource for those currently receiving counseling. I trust you will find this to be a practical, uplifting book that will provide you with hope and help as you approach concerns common to all of us. A wise prophet said, "All people, regardless of their background or circumstances, are capable of improving themselves." I know you can do it.

I wish you my best.

John R. Fishbein, Ph.D.

INTRODUCTION

To help you get the most value from this book, it will be helpful to review how it is organized. There are two general sections—Central Principles and Common Concerns.

Central Principles

Each principle is presented in a way designed to help you better understand and apply it in your life or in the lives of those you counsel. Information pertaining to each principle is organized into three parts:

- *General Information*: To help you better understand and apply the principle, practical information is provided.

- *Steps For Applying the Principle*: By taking the suggested steps, or at least the ones that apply to you, you will learn to apply the principle to whatever areas of your life you wish.

- *Personal Application*: Examples of clients successfully applying the principle are presented, giving you additional ideas on how to use the principle.

Common Concerns

Practical advice for solving personal problems (Communication Difficulties, Depression, Unsatisfactory Intimacy, and Anxiety Attacks) is presented in the following format:

- *Overview*: This section is designed not only to inform, but to put your concern in a solution-oriented perspective that is manageable and offers hope for success.

- *Barriers To Overcoming a Problem*: A number of barriers are presented, one or more of which are probably interfering with your efforts to overcome a problem. As you study the various barriers, you will find the following:

- *Common Indicators*: Thoughts, feelings, and actions commonly associated with each barrier are presented to help you identify the barrier(s) getting in your way. By reviewing the Common Indicators you will get an idea if a particular barrier is relevant to you.

- *General Information*: Practical information is provided to help you better understand and apply the principle.

- *Steps To Removing the Barrier*: By taking the suggested steps, or at least the ones that apply to you, you will be able to remove the barrier.

- *Success Story*: To give you additional ideas on how to apply the suggestions previously given, an account of a client successfully overcoming a problem is presented.

- *Summary*: A summary is provided to help you quickly review the key principles and actions necessary to overcome the problem.

How to Use this Book

Since *Emotional First Aid* is designed as a reference book there are a variety of ways to use it, depending on your needs and interests. One approach is to:

1. Select a common concern you would like to overcome or help someone else overcome.

2. Review the Central Principles. Identify the principle(s) not effectively being utilized. Take the appropriate steps to apply the principle(s).

3. Go to the section addressing the problem you wish to solve (Communication Difficulties, Depression, Unsatisfactory Intimacy, Anxiety Attacks).

4. Review the barriers to overcoming the problem. Identify the barrier(s) getting in the way. Take the appropriate steps to remove the barrier(s).

Some other ways to use this book include:

- Go to the section on the problem you wish to solve. Review the barriers to overcoming the problem. Identify the barrier(s) getting in the way. Take the appropriate steps to remove the barrier(s). Then, review the Central Principles.

- Study the Central Principles section to see how well you are applying the principles in general—without reference to any particular problem. Commend yourself for the principles you are effectively living. If you find a principle you would like to better apply, take the steps to do so.

- Browse through a section—Central Principles or Common Concerns—until you find a suggestion you would like to implement. Then, return in a week or so to look for another specific thing you can do to make positive progress.

- Study some or all of the book to learn more about solving personal problems.

- Give those you counsel (family member, church member, employee) an assignment to study and apply a particular part of the book; then, have them return and report their progress.

CENTRAL PRINCIPLES

1. **UNDERSTAND YOUR FEELINGS:** Emotions (also referred to as "feelings") are internal, physical-chemical sensations that provide you with important information about yourself, others, and your environment. Acknowledge your feelings, but use your head to make decisions.

2. **MANAGE YOUR THOUGHTS:** Every action and every feeling is preceded by thought, whether conscious or unconscious. Success and happiness, therefore, depend first and foremost on what you think. Strive to adhere to the Three Rules for Successful Thinking: Think Kindly, Think Objectively, and Think Constructively.

3. **DISTINGUISH YOUR FEELINGS FROM THE FACTS:** Feelings do not change facts. Strive to distinguish your feelings from the facts.

4. **FOCUS ON WHAT YOU CAN CONTROL RATHER THAN ON WHAT YOU CANNOT CONTROL:** In any situation there are things you can control and things you cannot control. Focus your attention on what you can control rather than on what you cannot control.

5. **RECOGNIZE YOUR INHERENT WORTH:** Feelings of self-worth fluctuate throughout life, but your intrinsic worth and identity is a God-given fact that is secure and permanent. You have value inherent in yourself independent of your feelings, your actions, or your accomplishments.

6. **BUILD A FIRM FOUNDATION FOR YOUR PERSONAL SECURITY:** Your security in life depends more on how you manage yourself than on any other person or thing.

7. **SET YOUR MINIMUM STANDARDS:** In any situation or relationship there are minimum requirements or standards you consider necessary for it to be acceptable (quite different from ideal or perfect.) While still striving to obtain the ideal, define your minimum standards. Measure quality or performance as being above or below your minimum acceptable standard.

8. **CARE FOR YOUR PHYSICAL HEALTH:** The health of your mind, body, and emotions depends on proper and consistent nutrition, exercise, and sleep. Strive to eat moderately, exercise regularly, and to get sufficient sleep.

   Rule of thumb: Eat three well-balanced, low-fat meals a day; exercise twenty to thirty minutes, three to four times a week; and sleep seven to nine hours a night.

UNDERSTAND YOUR FEELINGS

Emotions (also referred to as "feelings") are internal, physical–chemical sensations that provide you with important information about yourself, others, and your environment. Acknowledge your feelings, but use your head to make decisions.

GENERAL INFORMATION

Every thought that goes through your mind, whether conscious or unconscious, sends an important message to the body, which triggers a wave of internal motion (increased heart rate, blood pressure, body temperature, and muscle intensity). These internal, physical/chemical MOTIONS within the body are commonly felt and referred to as "eMOTIONS." Emotions are like a stream that is constantly flowing in each of us twenty-four hours a day. Sometimes the motion or flow is calm and tranquil; other times it is rapid and turbulent. Regardless of the nature of your stream of emotion at any given time, you—not the stream itself—make the decisions of what to think and how to act. Although it may not always seem like it, your behavior is controlled by the decisions you make, not by how you are feeling.

When you are upset, the agitation you feel in your body is the result of your mind triggering the release of chemicals, such as adrenaline, into your system (stream). On the other hand, when you think rational and happy thoughts, chemicals such as endorphins are released, causing you to feel good.

Unreasonable thinking—whether conscious or unconscious—pollutes the stream of emotion, thereby causing unpleasant feelings. Those feelings, like toxic chemicals dumped into a stream, eventually pass. How long it takes for them to pass, of course, depends on how long you continued to think unreasonably.

I am frequently asked, "How can a person control or get rid of undesirable feelings?" I often answer with the following question: "If you were camping by a stream and accidentally spilled gasoline into the water, what would you do?" Certainly, you would not jump into the stream and try to scoop the gas out. Nor would you chop down a tree to build a dam across the stream. Neither would you pretend the spill did not occur. How then would you deal with the gas spill? You would probably simply acknowledge you made a mistake, take precautions to avoid similar mistakes in the future, and perhaps warn the campers downstream to avoid swimming in the water till the spill passes. And it will pass!

A similar response is appropriate when you are feeling upset. Rather than ignoring or fighting upset feelings, simply acknowledge that they exist. Then look at yourself and the situation and decide what action, if any, to take.

> *Key Point*: When upsetting or toxic thoughts cause you to feel upset, the feelings will eventually pass as your thinking and behavior gets back on track.

DIFFERENCES BETWEEN EMOTIONAL BEHAVIOR AND EMOTION

It is easy to confuse emotional behavior, which is best controlled within some reasonable bounds, with emotion, itself. Although behavior such as fighting or fleeing may express emotion, it is not emotion itself. Emotion, for the most part, is simply the body's *internal* reaction to what is going on in the mind. It occurs internally as opposed to behavior which is external.

There is a distinct difference between the appropriate control of emotional behavior (controlling what you say or do when you feel angry) and the counterproductive attempt to control emotion (ignoring or fighting the feeling of anger). Although struggling to control the stream of emotion may seem natural, it is healthier to focus on and control the thoughts and actions that direct the stream, rather than focusing on the stream itself.

A DAMMED MISTAKE

Many people, when they are upset, make a common mistake. They futilely attempt to control, fight, or eliminate the stream of emotion. This results in the creation of a dam that blocks the natural flow of emotion, thereby causing unpleasant feelings to grow in magnitude and intensity. Rather than simply acknowledging whatever unpleasant emotions you are experiencing and finding a way to better manage yourself or your circumstances, you end up with compounded or dammed feelings. If you feel angry about something and then clog up your emotions, you end up with dammed anger in addition to the initial anger.

CONSCIOUS AND UNCONSCIOUS THOUGHTS

Your mind contains billions and billions of thoughts or pieces of information stored in the form of words or pictures. The thoughts you are aware of are referred to as conscious thoughts; they account for approximately 15%

THE STREAM OF EMOTION

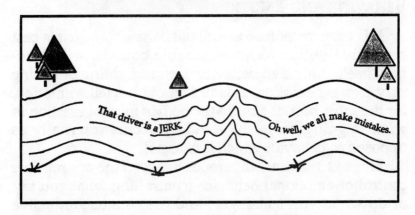

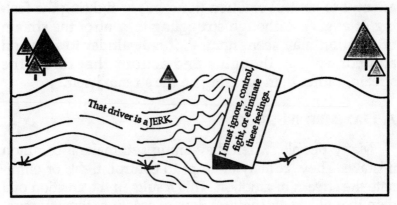

of mental activity. The other 85% of mental activity generally occurs without your awareness. The unconscious part of your mind automatically regulates breathing, heart rate, body temperature, digestion, etc.

Your unconscious mind also contains everything you have learned or experienced. It is like a great library containing vast quantities of information—some brain researchers suggest up to as many as 50 billion pieces of information. Of course, not every piece of information is readily available for recall, but each is nevertheless permanently recorded.

Situations, emotions, and conscious thoughts can trigger unconscious tapes or patterns of thinking. When you are driving an automobile, for example, and the highway situation changes, a tape containing everything previously learned about driving is triggered in your mind. This tape allows you to automatically speed up, slow down, or do whatever is necessary to safely meet the situation. This most likely occurs instantaneously, without any conscious thought or effort. Your conscious mind could even be involved with something entirely different, such as listening to the radio or daydreaming.

Your mind has many tapes like the one for driving, each containing valuable information or resources for effective living. Sometimes, however, these tapes and the solutions they contain seem to become forgotten and remain untapped. Other tapes contain outdated information, useful in the past but no longer applicable. Yet in some cases these tapes are silently interfering with current success and happiness. Still other tapes contain incomplete or irrational information causing unpleasant feelings and undesirable behavior. Some tapes are so powerful they can negatively interfere with your life, sometimes without you even being aware of the tape or of what it contains.

EMOTION—KEY TO THE MIND

How can you unlock the door to the vast library of learning contained in your mind? There is a key. Since every conscious or unconscious thought triggers a physical/chemical sensation, those emotions—pleasant or unpleasant—provide valuable feedback to what is going on in your mind. By learning to observe and use emotional information, you will discover better ways of managing yourself.

> *Key Point*: Your emotions are caused primarily by what goes on in your mind, not by any external situation. Likewise, what you do is determined by your mind, not by the emotions that may precede or accompany the behavior.

PURPOSE OF EMOTION

The *primary* purpose of emotion is to provide valuable information about what is going on in your mind—particularly your unconscious mind. If you feel peaceful, for instance, there is a good chance your thoughts are rational and productive; however, if you are feeling agitated, something in your mind probably needs attention.

Second, emotions provide important information about your behavior. If you are feeling calm, your behavior is likely to be purposeful and on track with your goals and values; on the other hand, uncomfortable feelings or agitation may be an internal indicator suggesting the need for careful examination of your behavior.

Third, emotions can provide useful clues about your physical health. If you are getting enough rest, proper nutrition, and regular exercise you will tend to feel well. Otherwise, your body may be telling you, via your emotions, to take better care of yourself.

Fourth, emotions can provide helpful information about your relationship with the Lord. When you are close to the Lord and in harmony with Him, you will tend to feel better and more peaceful than when you are further away.

When you are generally feeling well—with the usual emotional ups and downs—your thoughts, actions, physical health, and spirituality are most likely within reasonable guidelines and in balance. Intense or frequent emotional pain, however, usually suggests that some area of your life could benefit from attention and improvement. By paying attention to and understanding the important messages your body provides through emotion, you will gain greater self-mastery and happiness. When looked at in this manner, pain has a purpose and can be viewed constructively as "growing pain," rather than as a feared or hated enemy.

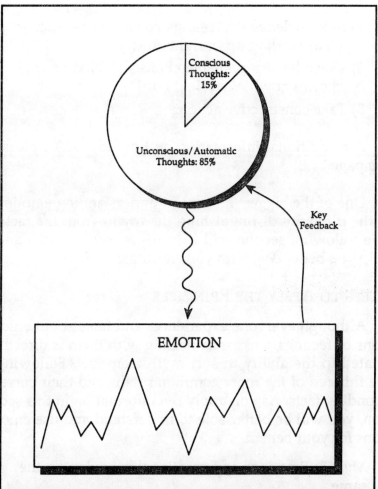

Important point: Emotion is primarily caused by what goes on in your mind, not by the situation that may have triggered the thoughts. Likewise, your behavior is caused by what occurs in your mind, not by the emotions that may precede or accompany the behavior.

TO BENEFIT FROM YOUR EMOTIONS—A.C. T.*

Rather than ignoring, dwelling on, or fighting your emotions, A.C.T:

1) **Acknowledge** the feelings you are experiencing ("I am feeling upset right now.")
2) **Consider** the available choices ("What are my choices now? What shall I do?")
3) **Take** constructive action.

For additional information on how to **A.C.T.**, please see page 149.

One of the biggest hurdles in understanding emotion is the difficulty distinguishing the myths from the facts. The following section will help dispel some myths and help you better deal with your feelings.

STEPS TO APPLY THE PRINCIPLE

Although everyone experiences and talks about emotions or feelings, success in dealing with them is directly related to the ability to sort myth from fact. Following are thirteen of the more common myths and their corresponding facts. As you apply the information in this section, you will be better able to understand and use emotions for your benefit.

Myth 1: Emotions and emotional behavior are the same.

Fact: Your behavior (laughing, crying, frowning, yelling, hitting . . .) may represent what you are feeling, but it is not the feeling itself. For instance, you can feel angry without acting angry.

---

* The idea for the acronym"A.C.T." came from *Rapid Relief from Emotional Distress*, Gary Emery and James Campbell. Ballantine Books, Inc., 1986.

Myth 2: Emotion must be controlled.

Fact: Your emotions provide you with useful information to help you better control your thoughts and your actions. Emotion itself, however, is not to be controlled. Trying to control, alter, or ignore your feelings is like putting tape over your car's instruments so you would not have to be bothered by them. By doing so you would miss out on valuable, even critical information, necessary to drive safely; you could get a speeding ticket—or your car might run out of gas or overheat.

By paying attention to your feelings—your emotional instruments—rather than trying to control them, you are in a better position to more effectively control yourself. *Result:* With better self-control you generally feel better.

Myth 3: Feeling that something is a fact makes it so.

Fact: Feelings do not change facts.

> *Example:* Feeling dumb does not change the fact you have a good mind. Feeling ugly does not change the fact you have a reasonably attractive body. Feeling like you are the greatest does not change the fact there are others who can do certain things better than you can.

Myth 4: You must do something to get your feelings out.

Fact: Feelings cannot be physically taken out of your body. You may describe what you are feeling: "I feel tense and agitated" or you may act in a way suggesting how you feel (clenched fist, raised voice, furrowed brow), but feelings, unlike a piece of food caught between your teeth, cannot be removed. Sometimes, however, talking about what you are feeling will bring about a feeling of relief—as though you were getting your feelings out.

Key point: There is a stream of emotion continuously ebbing and flowing through your body twenty-four hours a day. Fortunately (or unfortunately) whatever you are feeling at any given moment will eventually pass regardless of what you do.

Myth 5: The happiest most successful people follow their feelings.

Fact: The best decisions are usually made with 90% head and 10% heart—not the other way around. Emotion is designed to be a feedback mechanism, not a guidance system.

Myth 6: Analyzing the "why" of unpleasant feelings will make them go away.

Fact: The more you think about unpleasant feelings, the more intensely you are apt to feel them. It is better to acknowledge the feelings and say to yourself, "I am feeling upset." Then, rather than dwelling on the feelings, look for something constructive to do. Fortunately the unpleasant feelings, like an oil spill in a clear spring, will eventually pass.

Myth 7: Talking about unpleasant feelings is the best way to get rid of them.

Fact: There are certainly some benefits to talking (including the possibility of increased understanding of self and another, closer relationships, more objective thinking, and better perspective); however, talking does not automatically create the thoughts and actions necessary to feel better. What comes out of the mouth does not necessarily change what is in the mind.

> *Example:* Recklessly driving a car 75 m.p.h. and yelling, "I am going too fast" obviously does not change anything.

Myth 8: When emotionally upset, reasonable thinking will quickly produce better feelings.

Fact: Emotional pain, like physical pain, takes time to heal. An upsetting thought is like touching a hot stove. You can do so for a second or two without getting burned badly, but for every additional second, the degree of burn is worse and the time to heal is longer. The healing time for emotional pain is about ten times the amount of time you spent thinking the upsetting thoughts. The emotional pain from four minutes of upsetting thinking, for example, will take about forty minutes to heal.

Myth 9: Certain emotions should be eliminated.

Fact: Like water continuously flowing down a stream, emotion can be directed or redirected, but it cannot be shut off.

> *Example:* When you are feeling angry or depressed, you cannot simply turn off the stream of feelings because they are unpleasant. Unpleasant feelings always have a cause and that cause must be addressed and taken care of before you can feel better. Many artificial and unhealthy ways exist to seemingly turn off or dam up feelings (alcohol, drugs, food, T.V., etc.). However, the mind itself can produce chemicals or drugs—endorphins, for example—that can naturally have a powerful anesthetic or numbing effect on the body's feelings.

Myth 10: Emotions are illogical.

Fact: Emotion is your body's natural and logical

response to what is occurring in the mind. Although feelings may or may not be logically related to a situation, they are a logical reaction to what is occurring in your mind. Upsetting thoughts—whether conscious or unconscious—cause upset feelings and calm thoughts cause calm feelings.

Caution: Even though emotion logically follows thinking, thinking itself may or may not be logical.

Example: A person going deeper and deeper into debt may not feel any stress, because he is thinking, albeit illogically, that all is well.

Myth 11: Some people do not have feelings.

Fact: Everybody has feelings, whether expressed or not. Many people, however, have yet to learn how to express what they are feeling. Others have learned to ignore or even shut down their awareness of feelings, perhaps in a misguided attempt to protect themselves from emotional pain.

Myth 12: You should feel badly about feeling badly.

Fact: Telling yourself you are bad for feeling badly or that you should not have felt bad in the first place only serves to make you feel worse. It is better to take some corrective action or else ride out the emotional wave until you feel better.

Myth 13: Happy people do not feel much emotional pain.

Fact: To experience pleasure, you must also know pain. All people, from time to time, feel emotional pain, sometimes to extreme degrees. Although some people seem to experience less pain than others, unless we walk in their shoes, it is difficult to tell for sure the degree of pain they actually feel.

PERSONAL APPLICATION

Those who knew Ed at work or at church found him to be an intelligent and kind man, generally patient and tolerant of others' shortcomings. At home, however, so many things—especially little things—seemed to upset him. When his wife did not express herself well, for example, he became irritated or when his children repeatedly asked questions, he became impatient.

His wife, Jan, came to see me because she saw their fine family deteriorating. She thought maybe she was doing something to upset Ed, although she did not think so. She insulated him from as many of the family stresses as possible, hoping not to upset him. Despite her efforts, he was often upset.

I explained to her the nature of emotion, particularly how emotion is the body's chemical-physical reaction to what is occurring in the mind. I pointed out she and the children were responsible for their actions, *not* for Ed's reactions. That was somewhat hard for her to accept since Ed frequently said she and the children were responsible for upsetting him. I reassured her that although Ed may sincerely believe other people and events cause his emotional upsets, he was mistaken. He, not others, was responsible for how he felt.

Key point: Emotion is caused by the mind, *not* by outside events.

At our next meeting, Jan reported that an unusual thing had happened—Ed was feeling worse and she was feeling better. I asked her what she was doing differently. She explained the main difference was her understanding that he was responsible for his upsets, not her. She felt relieved. Nevertheless, she continued to be kind and considerate, although she did stop taking extraordinary measures to "protect" him from the things *he* upset himself about.

When he noticed he was feeling worse, while she was feeling better, he began thinking. "Perhaps," he wondered, "she is not the problem after all." He then came in to see me. He was not as receptive as Jan to the idea that he, rather than his environment, was responsible for his emotional upsets. I told him I would give him a powerful question to ask himself whenever he felt upset. I suggested to him that because he was an intelligent man he would soon know what caused his upset after he asked the question:

> *Did the Situation Upset Me?*
> *OR*
> *Did I Upset Myself?*

The next time I saw Ed, he told me he was not sure whether or not he liked the question. I detected a hint of a smile as he went on to explain what happened. One evening, while he and Jan were talking, the children burst into the living room arguing about something. He characteristically started to feel upset, when he noticed Jan dealing with the children in a calm and reasonable manner. He then bravely asked himself, "Did the situation upset me or did I upset myself?"

As he pondered the question, he thought about how he deals with employee problems at work. As a manager, it was not unusual for him to help angry employees solve conflicts with one another. It occurred to him that he rarely felt upset around employees who were thinking or acting unreasonably. "How can it be that I act so rationally at work and so irrationally at home?" he wondered. Then like a lightning bolt out of the sky, it hit him, "I am responsible for how I react to events around me."

Rather than looking for ways to change those around him at home, Ed began to look for ways to better manage himself. After the children left the room, he thoughtfully looked at Jan. He then asked her to help him understand what she does to act as rationally at home as he does at work.

Neither Jan or Ed could believe the changes that were taking place. Rather than blaming her for his upsets, he sought her advice. He began to be more reasonable and patient with the stresses of family life. He even called a family council and taught the family about the nature of emotion and what causes it. He even taught them the question he had learned.

Giving them the question turned out to be a blessing and a curse. One time when Ed was angry and arguing with his teenage daughter, he mistakenly told her she was making him mad. She wittily responded, "Dad, am I upsetting you or are you upsetting yourself?"

> **Reminder:** *If this central principle does not apply to your particular concern, go to another central principle or go directly to the section on the problem you wish to solve (Communication Difficulties, Depression, Unsatisfactory Intimacy, or Anxiety Attacks).*

CENTRAL PRINCIPLE 2

MANAGE YOUR THOUGHTS

Every action and every feeling is preceded by thought, whether conscious or unconscious. Success and happiness, therefore, depend first and foremost on what you think. Strive to adhere to the three rules for successful thinking: **think kindly, think objectively,** *and* **think constructively.**

GENERAL INFORMATION

Driving your car down the highway without lane lines to safely guide your way would be dangerous and frightening. Lane lines serve as guides to keep you on course to your destination. The mind is much more powerful and complex than the most sophisticated automobile. It can rapidly speed down any of billions of available highways. It can shift from one highway to another or change directions in a fraction of a second.

With the mind, as with a car, it is easy to believe you are correctly headed toward your destination, even when you are not. I remember one time I was happily driving south toward San Jose enjoying a lively conversation with a friend when I realized I was actually twenty miles north of home headed toward San Francisco. Because I thought I was on course and because I felt comfortable and happy, I had not paid enough attention to the road signs.

Because of the billions of roads or neural pathways in the mind and the computer-like speed with which thoughts travel and change directions, it is extremely easy to think you are headed north toward success and happiness when, in fact, you are drifting northeast or even south. Unfortunately many people evaluate their mental travels more by how their body feels rather than by the actual road they are traveling or by the direction they are headed. Without a well defined map and clearly marked road signs, it is all too easy to be misdirected or even lost.

There are many beneficial ways to manage the mind. To help keep your mind on a course headed toward success and happiness—where ever that happens to be for you—I suggest three basic rules or guidelines:

1. Think Kindly
2. Think Objectively
3. Think Constructively

All three rules, not just one or two, are essential for successful and happy living. When you think kindly *you* feel better regardless of how others are acting or feeling. When you think objectively you deal with facts in any given situation, even if they are not pleasant, which gives you the freedom to consider the best available choices. When you think constructively you focus on the things that are congruent with your goals and values.

To think objectively about your present situation without a clear idea of what you want to accomplish and how you plan to do it is not constructive. Likewise, to think objectively and constructively without thinking kindly toward others erodes the very essence of life—joy and love. Adherence to all three rules provides a safe and fertile environment to learn to live successfully and happily.

THINK KINDLY

To act in an unkind, disrespectful, or lustful way toward a person is obviously inappropriate and non-productive. To think such thoughts wastes valuable mental and emotional energy and also weakens the effectiveness of your mind. Your happiness and the quality of your relationships with others is increased or decreased, among other things, by how kindly you think. Consider a slight modification to The Golden Rule: *Think about others— including yourself—as you would have others think about you.*

Unkind thinking: Randy is selfish, inconsiderate, and no good.

Kind Thinking: Sometimes Randy is not as thoughtful as he could be.

Unkind thinking: What an idiot I am; I've forgotten her name again.

Kind Thinking: I have a reasonably good memory, so I must not have been paying attention when we were introduced or I would remember her name.

THINK OBJECTIVELY

As you think about any situation, your mind does two important things. First, it acts like a camera, recording the objective facts of the event. Then it acts like a news commentator analyzing and commenting on the recorded facts. As long as these two mental functions occur separately and in that order, your thinking is apt to be objective.

Confusing your opinions and feelings about an event with the objective "camera" facts interferes with your ability to think objectively. You end up with incomplete, inaccurate, or exaggerated information in your mind.

Key Point: No amount of intelligence can compensate for a lack of objective thinking.

Incorrect: My wife is always telling me what to do.

Objective Thinking: When my wife wants me to fix something around the house, she usually asks in a polite way. After the first five or six requests, however, she tends to get frustrated.

Incorrect: Unless I do what he wants, he gets angry at me.

Objective Thinking: Sometimes, when I don't do what he wants, he gets angry, period.

Although you could think, "He is mad *at me*," that thought will tend to cause you to interpret his feelings as a personal attack rather than as an expression of his thoughts or feelings, which probably have more to do with him than with you.

THE PROBLEM WITH SHOULD

A common barrier to thinking objectively is often created by how you use the "S" word—Should. If *should* means to you that what *is* must not or cannot be—rather than meaning you *prefer* reality to be different than it is—then the frequent use of the "S" word will upset you and fog your lenses. For example:

I shouldn't have dropped the ball.

Better: Unfortunately, I dropped the ball.

I should be as organized as Sue.

Better: Sue is more organized, but I can improve if I am willing to work at it.

Life shouldn't be so hard.

Better: At times life is hard, so what can I do to make my life better?

By thinking about life the way *it is* right now—even if you do not like it—you are in the best possible position to consider the available options and make your best choice.

THINK CONSTRUCTIVELY

Regardless of what you are doing, you are striving toward some goal or another, whether consciously or unconsciously. The mind is goal oriented. Right now, for example, as you read this, you have a reason, an objective, or a goal for doing so. There is something you want to accomplish. You may want to learn something, you may want to solve a problem, or you may just be curious about what is in this book. Likewise, when you talk to a friend or business associate, you have a purpose in mind. Even when you stare at the ceiling or out the window, you have your reasons. You may be pondering the solution to a difficult problem, you may be trying to relax for a moment, or you may be trying to avoid thinking about a particular problem or responsibility.

You *can* control the goals you think about and the plans you develop to accomplish them. You determine what goal, at any given moment, is most important to you. When you focus your mental energy on the goal you consider most important and when you focus your thoughts and activity on a reasonable plan to accomplish your goal, your mind is working at its best—constructively.

Incorrect: Why is my boss so impatient? I just can't seem to figure him out.

Constructive Thinking: Rather than asking "Why," ask, How can I do a better job and make my boss's job easier?

Incorrect: I cannot stand people driving slowly in the fast lane. I wish I had a Sherman tank.

Constructive Thinking: Although I do not like slow drivers in the fast lane, my main goal is to get home safely. Taking an extra five minutes to get there really doesn't matter. Also, I do have the option of driving around the slow drivers.

LEARNING TO ADHERE TO THE THREE RULES

Learning to keep your thoughts within a set of guidelines is like learning to drive an automobile between the white lines on the highway. It is easy now, because of years of practice, but remember that in the beginning it was not so easy. How did you do it?

First, you saw others driving safely in the appropriate lanes. You decided that was how you wanted to drive. Second, you practiced over and over again. Each time you made a mistake and drifted over the lane line, you quickly made a correction. Eventually, you became able to automatically keep your automobile centered between the lane lines, making little corrections whenever necessary, without consciously thinking about it.

Now it is easy to keep your automobile centered. Of course, you recognize the fact that everyone occasionally drifts and crosses the line—whether in an automobile or in their minds. You cannot always drive or think perfectly even though you give it your best effort. So when you do drift, you immediately *acknowledge* the fact you are out of line. You cannot afford to waste precious seconds criticizing yourself, questioning why, or disbelieving the fact you are out-of-bounds. And you certainly cannot afford to ignore the situation just because it is unpleasant. Instead, you simply and quickly act to *get back* in bounds. Finally, after you are safe, you think about and *learn* from your mistake.

In learning to manage your thoughts—striving to keep them within the bounds you set—the methods used are the same ones you used when learning to drive an automobile, or for that matter, to live within any guidelines you set (going to bed and getting up at a certain time, keeping social or work behavior within appropriate limits, and so forth). Just as it is obviously desirable to keep your car within the appropriate lines, so it is with your thoughts.

> *Key Point:* Strive to keep your thoughts within the Three Rules for Successful Thinking.

When your thoughts drift out of bounds—and they do for all of us—strive to *acknowledge* the thought and *get back* in bounds as quickly as possible—ideally within two to three seconds. Then there will be little or no negative emotional consequence.

> *Caution:* Sometimes an undesirable thought occurs without you noticing it right away.

> *Solution:* Regularly monitor and evaluate your thoughts by asking three questions:

> 1. *Am I thinking kindly?*
> 2. *Am I thinking objectively?*
> 3. *Am I thinking constructively?*

STEPS FOR APPLYING THE PRINCIPLE

1. Consider the benefits of adhering to the Three Rules for Successful Thinking. Ask yourself: "How will I benefit from learning to think this way?" Then consider whether the benefits are worth the effort. If so, decide that you will learn to live by the three rules—not because you have to or should, but because you want to.

2. Establish your own personal rules or guidelines for successful thinking. You may adopt the

three rules if you wish, or you may develop your own specific rules.

3. Evaluate your thoughts as desirable or undesirable, according to the rules you established. Make sure your line between desirable and undesirable thoughts is crystal clear, like the center divider line of a highway. In other words, make sure you understand what each of the three rules means in a personal and practical way.

Additional steps for managing undesirable thoughts are best understood by dividing them into three sections: 1) *before* undesirable thoughts occur, 2) *during* the occurrence of undesirable thoughts, and 3) *after* undesirable thoughts have occurred.

Before Undesirable Thoughts Occur:

1. Set a thinking goal you can immediately begin to succeed in accomplishing.

   Incorrect: I will *always* keep my thoughts within the guidelines I have set.

   Reason: A promise to always or never think certain thoughts is difficult if not impossible to keep; hence, you are apt to make yourself miserable and eventually give up.

   Correct: I will *learn* to keep my thoughts within the guidelines I set.

   Key Point: "I will learn" is a goal you can begin to succeed with immediately and continue for the rest of your life.

2. Involve yourself in a well-balanced variety of constructive activities (family, church, work, social, physical, school, music, service, etc.). If

your life is out of balance, you will have difficulty making any lasting improvements in controlling your thoughts.

3. Identify thoughts that in and of themselves are innocent but nevertheless tend to trigger or encourage undesirable thoughts. For instance, noticing and thinking about how attractive someone is, for just a few seconds, can be a harmless activity unless it subtly leads your mind out-of-bounds and causes you to lust after his or her body. Such 'innocent' thoughts are like a calm river that slowly and inevitably carries you towards raging rapids and dangerous falls.

4. Make a list of 'innocent' thoughts that tend to precede or trigger your undesirable thoughts. Then when you notice yourself thinking such thoughts, strive to immediately divert your attention to more constructive thoughts and activity. It is much easier to redirect your thinking when a potentially undesirable thought is in its infancy and still appears innocent.

5. Evaluate the relationships, conversations, and activities you participate in. Do they encourage or discourage you from keeping your thoughts within your guidelines? Also, consider the media smorgasbord you choose from (T.V., movies, radio, magazines, and books).

6. Make a list of situations or activities that tempt or encourage you to violate your rules for successful thinking. Begin decreasing, and if possible, eliminate your participation in such situations.

7. Develop a healthy mental diet, just as you do a physical diet. Feed your mind constructive, uplifting food. Avoid unhealthy thoughts as you would avoid unhealthy food. By reading uplifting and wholesome material, such as the scriptures, classic novels, biographies, and poetry, you will be strengthened in your efforts to better manage your thoughts.

Key point: What you feed your mind determines what kind of mind you will have.

DURING THE OCCURRENCE OF UNDESIRABLE THOUGHTS

1. To better understand the nature of the undesirable thoughts you are striving to control, bridle, or redirect, consider the following similes:

- Dirty, rotten thoughts are like trash. You can put them in a trash can and even take them to the dump, but you cannot entirely eliminate or forget them. When properly disposed and treated, however, trashy thoughts cease to stink up or disturb the mind.

- Continuing to think undesirable thoughts is like throwing wood on a campfire (your emotions). For every additional second you entertain an upsetting thought, the emotions burn more brightly. Attempting to battle or analyze undesirable thoughts is like trying to put out the fire by blowing on it: the fire burns brighter and the coals burn hotter. It is better to step back and stop throwing wood on the fire. Do something else. Let the emotional fire die on its own.

- An undesirable thought is like a snowball rolling down a hill. At first it is small and easy to manage, but as it continues to roll it grows and builds momentum, eventually becoming difficult to stop.

• Undesirable thoughts are like inappropriate requests or comments an attorney makes in court. The judge can instruct the jury to disregard them. You, like the judge, can overrule any thought or resulting feeling by instructing your mind to disregard it. Although you cannot entirely erase the memory of the thoughts or the feelings they produce, you do not have to take them seriously or act on them.

• However, trying to make yourself NOT think a particular thought is like trying NOT to think about pink elephants or trying to forget a song you heard a thousand times. Such an impossible—or at least highly unlikely—goal becomes even more difficult when you are afraid. Just imagine if someone threatened to shoot you if you ever thought about or felt like thinking about pink elephants again. Instead, when you think an undesirable thought—and we all do from time to time—immediately acknowledge what you are thinking. Then immediately redirect your thinking to something kind, objective, and constructive.

• Sometimes a set of thoughts, beliefs, or memories are so powerful and pervasive (such as deeply rooted beliefs about not being good enough, upsetting sexual thoughts and memories or anxiety-producing thoughts and memories) that they keep reoccurring like a chronic illness. They tend to haunt the mind with flashbacks and waves of undesirable feelings. Although such toxic thoughts may not be entirely eliminated, with a great deal of effort and vigilance they can be decreased, desensitized, and put into remission where they no longer interfere with your ability to live the way you choose.

2. When you think an undesirable thought, take two key steps:

Step One: Immediately *acknowledge* the fact that your thoughts are out-of-bounds. *Reason*: Ignoring undesirable thoughts is like ignoring weeds in your garden. You may temporarily feel better by pretending the weeds do not exist, but they will grow and spread just the same. When they become so large and numerous that ignoring them is impossible, control becomes extremely difficult.

Step Two: Immediately redirect or refocus your attention and activity on something constructive despite any powerful, lingering feelings that may occur. Do not attempt to fight or stop the thought itself.

Reason: Emotionally charged thoughts, like a powerful freight train, cannot be stopped dead in their tracks. You can however, change the destination of a train—or a train of thought—by switching the tracks.

Example: Even after the train is stopped, the hot wheels (emotions) do not immediately cool off. Just as the train engine produces power and heat to drive the wheels, your thoughts produce chemicals that create physical/emotional sensations you feel in your body.

Caution: After you get your thoughts back in bounds, be patient with your emotions. Give them time to cool off. Do not go back out-of-bounds in a misguided attempt to fight or analyze the undesirable thoughts or feelings.

Note: If strong feelings are associated with a particular undesirable thought, it is better to find something you can actively do (such as work on a project exercise or call a friend) rather than just trying to get rid of the feeling or thought by thinking about something else.

3. Practice the previous two steps (acknowledge and redirect your thoughts) until you can consistently do both within two to three seconds. That may be difficult at first, but by practicing— hundreds of times if necessary—you will succeed. See the diagram on the following page.

Note: The longer your thoughts are out-of-bounds, the stronger the pull to continue dwelling on them.

4. Notice how the intensity and duration of undesirable feelings decreases as you decrease the amount of time your thoughts are out-of-bounds.

AFTER UNDESIRABLE THOUGHTS HAVE OCCURRED

1. Even after you have your thoughts back in bounds, be patient with the way you feel. The length of time it takes your body to calm down after having undesirable sexual, anxious, angry, or depressing thoughts is about ten times as long as the time your thoughts were out-of-bounds.

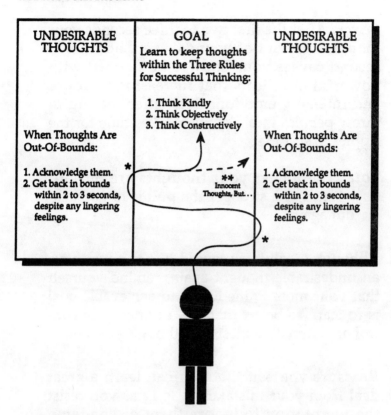

* As you become more skilled in keeping your thoughts within the Three Rules—or quickly getting your thoughts back in bounds when they drift—two important results occur: you think more effectively, and you tend to feel better—sooner or later.

** As you identify and avoid thoughts that, in and of themselves, are innocent but tend to lead to undesirable thoughts, it is much easier to stay within the guidelines.

Reason: After the first two to three seconds your thoughts are out-of-bounds, every additional second causes your body to be flooded with powerful chemicals that increasingly arouse and intensify emotion. Even after ceasing to throw pebbles into a pond, it takes time for the ripples to subside.

> *Note*: The longer your thoughts are out-of-bounds, the stronger the pull is to go back out again.

2. Although ideally you would like to never have an undesirable thought again, remind yourself that your more immediate and achievable goal is to learn to better manage, not perfectly control or eliminate undesirable thoughts.

3. Reassure yourself that you can learn a great deal from your mistakes as long as you resist the temptation to ignore them or condemn yourself for having made them in the first place.

> Ask yourself:
>
> *"With hindsight, what could I have done to prevent my thoughts from going out-of-bounds in the first place?"*
>
> *"What could I have done once my thoughts were out-of-bounds to more quickly acknowledge and correct them?"*

4. Think about what you can learn from your mistakes that will help you do better next time.

5. Instead of just trying to learn from your mistakes, think of some of the times you were tempted to think an undesirable thought but instead thought about something else. Think about how you did it. Ask yourself what was different during those times.

Example: Larry asked me to help him not get so angry at other drivers. He had spent a great deal of time analyzing—to no avail—why he became irate when someone else was driving incorrectly or inconsiderately. I gave him what seemed to be an unusual assignment. I asked him to watch for situations he could have been upset about but was not. Then I asked him to figure out what he was thinking or doing that allowed him *not* to feel so upset.

Key point: Too often people spend more time dwelling on their mistakes than on analyzing and learning from their successes.

6. After making and correcting a mistake, recommit yourself to your goal (say to yourself, "I will learn to keep my thoughts within the guidelines I've set, no matter how long it takes").

7. Frequently review your reasons for choosing to learn to keep your thoughts within the guidelines you set. Doing so will reaffirm your desire for greater peace of mind, more happiness, and increased personal productivity.

You may wish to study the chart on the following pages to gain a clearer overview of the three different areas of managing undesirable thoughts.

Managing Undesirable Thoughts

BEFORE THEY OCCUR

GOAL: Prevention

METHOD:

1. Increase constructive activity designed to keep your life in balance.
2. Avoid tempting situations.
3. Become aware of and avoid seemingly innocent thoughts and activities which nevertheless precede or trigger undesirable thoughts.

RESULT:

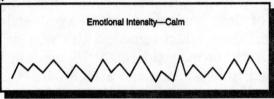

Emotional Intensity—Calm

WHEN THEY OCCUR

GOAL: Correction

METHOD:

1. Acknowledge and accept the existence of undesirable thoughts.
2. Get your thoughts back in bounds as quickly as possible (Ideal: 2 to 3 seconds) by focusing your thoughts and activities on something constructive, despite any lingering feelings to the contrary.

RESULT:

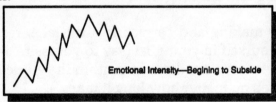

Emotional Intensity—Begining to Subside

AFTER THEY OCCUR

GOAL: Learn from the experience

METHOD:

1. Be patient with any lingering, undesirable feelings.
2. Do not condemn yourself for having some undesirable thoughts.
3. Reassure yourself that you can learn a great deal from your mistakes.
4. Think about how you can do better next time.

RESULT:

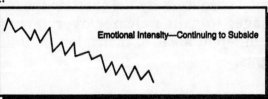

Emotional Intensity—Continuing to Subside

PERSONAL APPLICATION

Since he was thirteen years old, Sean struggled unsuccessfully to overcome a habit of sexual behavior that violated his personal and religious values (masturbation). As he told me of his efforts I listened to how he dealt with the two key factors occurring in any problem—his behavior and his thoughts.

Note: The principles and strategies used to help Sean can be applied to any habit you wish to overcome.

"I'LL NEVER DO IT AGAIN"—A SELF-DEFEATING PROMISE

Exception: If Sean was dealing with a mistake he made once or twice—rather than habitually—it would have been all right to promise to never do it again. *Reason:* Before the behavior developed into a habit, he would probably have been able to keep his promise. However, with any well-established habit, a different approach is essential.

Sean tried a variety of strategies to eliminate the undesirable behavior. With each new approach, he sincerely promised himself the same thing: "I'll never do it again." He would psyche himself up, sure that this time he would finally succeed. He kept records of how many days in a row he went without a "slip." One day, two days, a week, two weeks, and so forth. The longer he went, the more the pressure built—"How long can I keep it up? Have I finally overcome it?" Then, inevitably, the winning streak came to an end.

The first few dozen times he promised "to never do it again" and failed, he dusted himself off and tried again. Eventually, however, he began to doubt himself: "I don't know if I can overcome this problem. Maybe I am a loser. If others knew about my problem, they would think less of me. I'm a phony. Even God is displeased with me."

Despite increasing doubt and discouragement he never gave up. He kept fighting.

A VICIOUS CYCLE DEVELOPS

Realizing his thoughts were at the root of his behavior, he began fighting them. His goal: *eliminate* lustful thoughts. When a lustful thought came into his mind, he attacked it like a general trying to destroy the enemy. He tried to *force* it out of his mind by screaming to himself, "No!" and by repeating positive affirmations, or by trying to frighten himself about possible future consequences of his actions. He would hold the thought up for careful analysis, asking himself "why" he thought such things. At other times he would wage a mighty debate trying to convince himself he did not want to think those thoughts.

Sean was caught in a vicious cycle. The harder he tried to battle his thoughts and make them go away, the more they tended to dominate his thinking. It was like trying NOT to think about purple alligators. The more he thought about NOT thinking certain things, the more he was actually thinking about them.

In addition to failing to keep his promise of "never doing it again," he was also failing in his fight to "eliminate undesirable thoughts." Failure was uppermost in his mind.

REACHING OUT FOR HELP

By the time Sean came to see me, needless to say, he was discouraged. He was down on himself and doubted his own ability to succeed. He looked to me to do something to solve his problem. My first objective was to help him discover that the solution was still within him.

We discussed his goal "to never do it again," and I asked him how he would know when he had succeeded. He said, "When I don't do it anymore." I asked him how many days in a row he thought he needed to go before he could reach that conclusion. He said he really didn't know, but thought it needed to be a long time, perhaps a year.

I pointed out that his criteria for success was vague at best and nonexistent at worst. Unless he could say he never made a mistake, he could not say he succeeded. And how could he conclude "I never make a mistake" when he does not know what the future holds.

> *Key point:* Because he could not objectively measure progress, let alone success, he was frequently anxious or discouraged, thereby making learning difficult. His goal, though well-meaning and sincere, was self-defeating.

SETTING AN ACHIEVABLE GOAL

I explained to Sean that he could set a different goal—a goal that would allow him to objectively recognize and measure progress. He would then be able to experience degrees of success that would be encouraging and lead to further success. I suggested the following goal:

> *I will learn to keep my passions within the bounds the Lord and I have set.*

There are two important parts to this goal. First, is the concept of *learning*. By focusing on *learning* he could experience some success right away. We discussed how people learn new skills such as riding a bike, playing basketball, or speaking a foreign language. It was obvious to him that learning new skills always involved making some mistakes, especially in the beginning. More important than the mistakes, however, is what you learn from them. I reassured him that although I understood his desire to get to the point where he could better control his thoughts and behavior, he must first *learn* the necessary skills. That means making some mistakes—and then learning from them.

> *Key Point:* Whenever you set a goal to develop a new habit, begin with the words, "I will learn to . . ."

I was careful to make sure he understood what I was saying. I had no intent whatsoever to encourage him to do anything he considered wrong or to mitigate the seriousness of his mistakes. I knew, nevertheless, that with well developed habits of many years, growing pains and mistakes were inevitable.

The second essential part of the goal is setting a positive orientation. The emphasis is on learning to do a positive thing, rather than on *not* doing a negative thing.

Positive: I will learn to hit the ball.

Negative: I will not strike out.

Positive: I will learn to obey the Lord.

Negative: I will not sin.

Key Point: You are more likely to succeed with a positive goal stating what you wish to accomplish, than a negative goal emphasizing what you do NOT want to do.

Sean agreed to adopt the new goal. Now he had a positive goal that allowed for the natural process of learning. I told him the next time we met, I would be more interested in what he learned than in whether or not he made a mistake. That took a lot of pressure off. I knew as long as he was learning principles and skills for better self-management—even amidst making some mistakes—he would sooner or later, gain greater control over his thoughts and his actions. Hence, he would soon be making fewer mistakes.

REAFFIRMING SELF-WORTH AMIDST MISTAKES

Sean had another habit that was getting in the way of accomplishing his goal. When he made a mistake he would get extremely down on himself. By repeatedly saying negative and unkind things about himself, he was making a second mistake. Without realizing it, he was causing the erosion of his natural sense of self-worth.

In order to shore up his self-esteem, I suggested he do something that initially seemed strange and awkward. I asked him to use his undesirable behavior to remind him to reaffirm his inherent, God-given worth. Just after he made a mistake, I asked him to recite the following words to himself: "I am a child of God with strengths, weaknesses, and potential. And I will *learn* to keep my passions within the bounds the Lord and I have set." Not only does the undesirable behavior reinforce correct principles, it usually becomes less desirable itself.

Keeping Objective Records

In solving any personal problem, I look for improvement in two areas—what a person thinks and how they behave. I showed Sean how to measure progress in those areas in a way that would be objective and encouraging.

In the area of measuring his behavior, rather than counting the days until he make a mistake, I suggested he keep a win/loss record. After the first week Sean reported he messed up two times. He was discouraged. My response was, "Well let's see, you have five wins and two loses. What did you learn?"

After the second week Sean was pleased to announce he made some progress. He reported a cumulative score for the two weeks of eleven wins and three loses. The progress was not only obvious, it was encouraging. Besides, he continued to learn important lessons about governing himself.

Next, to measure progress in keeping his thoughts within the bounds he set, I suggested two things. First, I asked him to monitor how many seconds or minutes it took him to (a) acknowledge that his thoughts were out-of-bounds and (b) get his thoughts back in bounds. Second, I asked him to make a list of "innocent" thoughts that, nevertheless, tended to lead his mind out-of-bounds ("She is cute" or "I need to relax"). Then I asked him to report the number of times he started down the track of "innocent" thoughts and then switched to a better track before he went out-of-bounds.

At first he had some difficulty recognizing the onset of his undesirable thoughts. He would be aware of his emotional reaction to the thoughts before he was aware of the thoughts themselves. I pointed out that by then the waves of emotion were so large it was difficult to redirect the wayward thoughts. When he finally got his thoughts back in bounds, he was in for a surprise—the feelings did not subside right away. I explained that for every second his thoughts were out of bounds, it usually takes about ten times that long for the body to completely calm down.

With practice, he got to the point where he could recognize an undesirable thought and get back in bounds in about a minute. Then he could do it in forty-five seconds; then thirty seconds. Sometimes, he could even do it in the ideal time of two to three seconds.

PREVENTION IS EASIER THAN CORRECTION

Sean learned prevention was easier than correction. By increasing his awareness of the "innocent" thoughts preceding the undesirable thoughts, he discovered he could comfortably redirect his thoughts *before* they got out-of-bounds. As he noted increasing success in keeping his thoughts in bounds, as well as quickly getting them back in bounds when they drifted, his confidence grew.

To help him gain greater confidence and strength, I asked him to consider others areas in his life he would like to improve (physical, social, intellectual, career, spiritual, service, and so forth). I explained that *anything* he could do to live a more meaningful and well-balanced life would help him solve his problem as well as reduce the likelihood of a recurrence.

At our last visit, Sean thanked me for helping him discover that all along he had had the power in himself to solve his problem. He also acknowledged the Lord's help. My experience with Sean brought to mind the example of a talented and dedicated football player who was running with all his might, only to discover he was going the wrong way. Sean just needed a little guidance to get himself pointed in the right direction.

> **Reminder:** *If this central principle does not apply to your particular concern, go to another central principle OR go directly to the section on the problem you wish to solve: Communication Difficulties, Depression, Unsatisfactory Intimacy, or Anxiety Attacks.*

DISTINGUISH YOUR FEELINGS FROM THE FACTS

Feelings do not change facts. Strive to distinguish your feelings from the facts.

GENERAL INFORMATION

All of us, from time to time, unwittingly blend our opinions or feelings with the facts and consider the resulting viewpoint to be the actual fact. You may think, for instance, that you are discussing the facts of a situation when you are actually talking about your own imagined version of the facts. The thoughts and feelings you have about a situation are, of course, important; nevertheless, they do not change this fundamentally important principle: Thoughts and feelings, no matter how sincere or strong, do not change the facts.

Although feelings can provide important and useful information, sometimes they give inaccurate or exaggerated information. In any situation, for instance, there are objective facts unaltered by personal opinion or feeling as well as subjective opinions and feelings. When you have a strong feeling (a feeling that all is well or all is lost) it is tempting to believe that the feeling itself accurately reflects reality. Sometimes, of course, what you feel is consistent with the facts of reality. At other times, however, what you feel may not be supported by the facts. In other words, feelings are not necessarily related to reality.

Distinguishing thoughts and feelings from facts can be better understood by considering how a camera works. A camera simply records facts as they are. It does not record personal thoughts or feelings. Unlike a camera, your mind can add opinions, assumptions, and feelings to the facts creating a customized picture—whether accurate or not—of any given situation. This is natural and healthy as long as the opinions and feelings are not thought of as the objective facts.

There are two ways of dealing with feelings that produce a distorted picture. At one extreme is the person who ignores his feelings altogether; at the other extreme is the person who excessively dwells on his feelings.

IGNORING FEELINGS

Although you can go through the motions of life while ignoring some or all of your emotions, you will be at a disadvantage. If you attempt to ignore emotional pain, for example, you will likewise have difficulty being sensitive to pleasure. Ignoring emotion also causes you to miss out on important information about yourself and your environment, making it difficult to think objectively, make reasonable decisions, or effectively communicate.

Missing out on the information provided by your emotions is like driving a car without paying attention to the instruments. You can still drive, but you are apt to make little mistakes like occasionally driving too fast, running out of gas, or overheating the engine. Likewise, without essential emotional information you are apt to make mistakes or get stuck while attempting to solve personal and relationship problems.

Some people, unaware of their feelings, mistakenly consider themselves highly rational. Such individuals often appear impeccably calm and smooth. Nothing seems to upset them. Like the automobile driver who ignores the fuel gauge registering empty while *thinking* and *acting* as though he has plenty of gas, some people ignore their emotional instruments, *thinking* and *acting* as if they were calm. If you are married to someone like that—and you are aware of your own normal emotional ups and downs—you (and he) may mistakenly view him as calm and yourself as volatile.

Contrary to outer appearances, the so-called "rational" man often has difficulty distinguishing facts from feelings because he is unaware that there is any difference between the two.

> *Example:* When Bill walked through the front door, Sharon knew he was upset. Bill, however, considered himself calm and rational. Actually Bill was upset about work but had not yet recognized that fact. When Sharon asked him how he was, he responded sincerely, "Fine." Upon looking around the house Bill launched into a tirade about how messy it was even though it was reasonably tidy. Because Bill was unaware of his feelings about work, he had difficulty seeing that the house was neat and that the problem lay within his own unrecognized feelings. His opinions were being affected by feelings he did not admit he had.

> *Key Point:* The truly rational person is aware of his feelings as clearly as he is aware of the facts in a situation.

DWELLING ON FEELINGS

Some people are so aware of and involved with their feelings that they lose sight of what the facts are and whether or not their feelings are supported by the facts.

Such individuals tend to base their opinions and decisions on how they feel, often without considering all of the facts in the situation. To them, what they feel represents what is real.

Attempting to reason or communicate with someone who believes that what they feel determines what is real is an exercise in frustration. They tend to give their feelings more credibility than the facts, regardless of how much evidence you give them. For example, although Norm and Sue are living beyond their means, when Norm *feels* they can afford a new car, financial facts cannot convince him otherwise. Since he *feels* good about the purchase, he "reasons," it must be all right.

> *Key point:* Thoughts and feelings do not change facts.

When you are able to distinguish the facts in a situation from your feelings about the facts, you are in the best position to objectively and sensitively examine all available information.

STEPS TO APPLYING THE PRINCIPLE

1. Practice reminding yourself of the key principle:

> *Thoughts and feelings do not change facts.*

- On several 3x5 cards write the above principle. Place the cards where you can see them at least a dozen times a day (refrigerator, T.V., mirror, visor of your automobile, etc.).

- Whenever you have a strong feeling or opinion, remind yourself of what is written on your cards.

2. When you experience a feeling that seems unreasonably strong or inappropriate to the situation, ask yourself:

> *"What are the facts that support this feeling?"*

Key point: When a particular feeling is not supported by facts, you are usually better off not taking it seriously. Acknowledge but do not dwell upon such feelings.

Caution: Even though feelings do not change facts, dwelling on feelings inconsistent with the facts creates the illusion that the feelings, nevertheless, represent truth and fact.

3. Practice distinguishing feelings from facts in three important areas of your life: Your identity ("I am" versus "I feel I am"), your activities ("I do" versus "I feel I do"), and your possessions ("I have" versus "I feel I have"). It helps to take a piece of paper and draw a line vertically down the center. List your feelings on the left side and the facts on the right side. See the example on the following page.

4. When there is a discrepancy between the facts and your feelings, you are usually better off acting on the facts rather than on your feelings. Emotions are usually not as reliable as the facts, since emotions can fluctuate independently of the current situation because of flashbacks from the past, exaggerated thoughts about the present or future, or insufficient information.

Feelings versus Facts

Identity

I *feel* . . .	I *am* (the facts)
I am worthless	me
I am great	Sharon
I am hopeless	a child of God with
I am brilliant	strengths weak-
I am a crumb	nesses, and poten-
I am a jerk	tial
I am a terrible per-son	female

Activity

I *feel* I do . . .	I *do* (the facts)
nothing good, im-portant, or worth-while.	take care of my family
everything perfect and right	community and church service
	regular exercise
	eat healthy food

Possessions

I *feel* I have	I *have* (the facts)
nothing of value	a family
no friends	friends
no money	job
	Church member-ship
	a house
	a car

PERSONAL APPLICATION

Terri, a high school homecoming queen, sincerely *felt* ugly and unpopular. Her parents repeatedly tried to reason with her but to no avail. Every time they pointed out the facts that over one thousand of her peers voted her homecoming queen and that she modeled for Macy's, she told them those things did not change her feelings.

I pointed out to Terri that her feelings were screaming so loudly in her ears, she mistakenly believed them to represent truth and reality. Her feelings were discoloring her view of the facts. Her parents, on the other hand, were so focused on the facts, they could not seem to acknowledge, let alone understand, her feelings.

I encouraged her parents to stop trying to use facts to talk her out of her feelings; instead, it would be better to acknowledge and respect her feelings even though they were not based on facts. I suggested they tell her they understood she was feeling down on herself. Then they could reassure her that the emotional storm would eventually pass.

Meanwhile, Terri and I discussed a variety of situations where feelings and facts are not one and the same, such as feeling like you failed a math test when in fact you did well or vice versa. She began to realize that although her feelings were real and understandable (we all feel badly about ourselves from time to time), those feelings do not change the facts.

Finally, the light went on—she saw that feeling down on herself did not change the fact that she did, indeed, have some positive physical characteristics and good friends. Once again, she was able to objectively look at her strengths and weaknesses independently of how she was feeling. The storm passed.

THUNDER FEELS SCARY—BUT IT IS NOT DANGEROUS

One afternoon we experienced an unusual thunderstorm in San Jose. We were so excited, we went outside to watch the lightning and listen to the thunder. Our young son, Chad, who ventured out with us felt differently. Although he was fascinated by the lightning, he jumped and shuddered with fear each time the thunder boomed.

Although I explained to him several times that thunder could not hurt him, his feelings were so strong that he was not convinced. The irony of the situation was that lightning—which Chad felt very safe and comfortable with—could be dangerous, while thunder—which was not dangerous—felt dangerous to him. I empathized with Chad because a couple of times the roar of thunder was so loud, I too jumped even though I *knew* there was no danger.

Key point: Feelings, no matter how strong, do not change the facts.

Reminder: *If this central principle does not apply to your particular concern, go to another central principle OR go directly to the section on the problem you wish to solve: Communication Difficulties, Depression, Unsatisfactory Intimacy, or Anxiety Attacks.*

WHAT YOU CAN VERSUS WHAT YOU CANNOT CONTROL

In any situation, there are things you can control and things you cannot control. Focus your attention on what you can control rather than on what you cannot control.

GENERAL INFORMATION

Although in every situation there are things you can control, there are also things you cannot control, no matter how much you may wish you could. For example, you may wish to turn sickness into health, make a bad driver good, make a hot day cool, make a depressed economy robust, make a noncommunicative spouse communicate, or make a disobedient child obey. The tendency to dwell on things you cannot control is normal and natural but unhealthy. It leads to feelings of anxiety, anger, or depression.

In personal relationships, thinking about things you cannot control often leads to manipulative behavior, whether consciously or unconsciously.

Key point: One of the biggest causes of relationship difficulties at home or a work is one person attempting to control another. Not only does the mind function poorly when dwelling on things you cannot control, relationships cannot prosper when one person attempts to inappropriately control the other.

The line between what you can and cannot control is often thin and easily overlooked. For instance, the Golden Rule can be misinterpreted to mean: "*If* I do unto others as I would have them do unto me, *then* they will do unto me as I want." Such a restatement suggests one person can control what another will choose to do. Certainly, if you are kind to others, there is a greater likelihood others will *choose* to reciprocate, but of course that is their choice, not yours.

Although there are physical or scientific laws that show an if-then, cause-and-effect, or stimulus-response relationship, people *choose* how they will act or respond. In human relationships, *if* you do something, *then* there may be a possibility, or even a probability of a certain response by the other person, but that choice is in his control, not yours.

Myth: Do unto others as you would have them do unto you, and they will do what you want. The problem occurs when you assume that your choices will cause another person to make the choice you want them to make.

Fact: Do unto others as you would have them do unto you, and they will more likely—though not necessarily—choose to do what you want.

Although optimum mental and emotional effectiveness is obtained by focusing approximately 90% of your attention and energy on what you can control, there are also things you cannot completely control that require your attention. Goals or plans involving other people or external events, for instance, are important to think about even though you cannot entirely control the outcome. For example, you may set a family goal to improve communication by speaking in a kind manner. Although you can control your contribution to the goal, better family communication requires the efforts of others, whom you cannot control.

Whether in a family or business setting, it is essential to have a clear goal, mission, or purpose, even though you alone cannot completely control the outcome. I suggest giving about 10% of your attention to important things you cannot control, such as goals, expectations, hopes, and dreams. But focus the vast majority of your attention (approximately 90%) on the things you can control: your contribution, effort, performance, thoughts, and feelings.

> *Result:* Within the limits of any given situation, you will experience optimum freedom and opportunity to be at your best, regardless of the people or things you cannot control. The outcome or product will be the result of the interweaving of your contribution with other variables such as other's contributions or lack of contribution, environmental, economic, mechanical factors, and so forth.

You Can Control	You Cannot Control
Your thoughts	The emotional consequences of your thoughts
Your choices	
Your actions	The consequences of your choices
Your influence on others, whether positive or negative	Others' reactions
Family rules and consequences for obedience or disobedience	Others' response to your influence
	Children's' choice to obey or disobey
Your effort, contribution, and performance at work	

There are some difficult or painful situations where desirable choices *seem* nonexistent (severe illness, deteriorating marriage and family relationships, or loss of job). In such cases, there is a natural tendency to give most, if not all, of your attention to the things you cannot control. This results in reduced awareness of available choices and in feeling trapped. Fortunately, the important fact remains that in *all* situations there are some constructive choices available—just not always the ones you might prefer.

A classic example of finding constructive choices in a situation that was anything but ideal is found in Dr. Viktor Frankl's experience in Auschwitz—a Nazi concentration camp where thousands of his fellow Jews, including his family, were murdered in the gas showers. Daily he saw the black smoke from the incinerated bodies rising to the sky. He was starved and tortured. Many of his fellow prisoners were dropping dead from starvation and despair. Did he have any positive choices? What could he control?

He made a remarkable discovery. Although the Nazis could take his family, possessions, and liberty, they could not take away his faith in God, his hopes and dreams, and his love for his fellow man. They could not make him hate or give up hope. Despite the atrocious conditions, he realized he could still do some good with his life. Regardless of how long he lived or under what conditions, he could help his fellow prisoners; he could learn to suffer with dignity. He could hope for and plan for a better life someday—even though the chance of survival was remote.

He found meaning and purpose in his life as he determined he would live to the best of his ability within the limits of his current circumstances. He discovered freedom in a Nazi concentration camp.

Although Dr. Frankl was certainly aware of things he could not control, he still found a way to focus his attention and energy on what he could control. As a result, he not only survived Auschwitz, he discovered freedom and meaning in his life; he also developed an internationally renowned theory and approach to psychotherapy, largely derived from his experience. (*Man's Search For Meaning*, Viktor E. Frankl, Washington Square Press, 1985).

When I am feeling down or upset about things I cannot control, I often think about Victor Frankl. If he could find peace of mind and meaning amidst the horrors of Auschwitz, I can certainly find a constructive way to cope with my challenges.

Although every situation contains people, things, or events you cannot control, constructive choices are available. When you focus attention on the things you cannot control, the result is apt to be emotional agitation and mental inefficiency. When you focus your attention on things you can control, however, you can think and feel at your best.

STEPS FOR APPLYING THE PRINCIPLE

1. When you come upon a difficult situation (either face-to-face or in your mind), consider what you can control versus what you cannot control.

> Ask yourself:
>
> *"What aspects of this situation can I control? What aspects can't I control? "*

Result: Just by asking the question and thinking about it, there is a natural tendency for your mind to self-correct.

2. When you find yourself dwelling on something you cannot control, do not try to change your thinking at first. Just watch what happens.

Observe the consequences, especially how you tend to feel and act.

Result: By increasing your awareness of what you are focusing on and the results that follow, your mind will naturally tend to focus more on things you can control.

3. Since feeling upset often indicates that you are thinking about things you cannot control, use your unpleasant feelings to remind you to ask the question on page 52.

4. To further distinguish between what you can and cannot control, take a piece of paper and draw a line down the center of the paper. On one side of the line write those aspects of the situation you can control and on the other side of the line write the aspects you cannot control.

Result: As you more clearly distinguish what you can control from what you cannot control, you will be able to better concentrate your energy and resources where you can do the most good.

5. Select one thing on your list you can control and implement a plan for doing something about it.

Example: A young mother of three children related to me how she felt overwhelmed, inadequate, and depressed. I told her my wife and I could personally relate with how she was feeling. She explained that in the last week alone, her six-year-old had screamed "I hate you" several times, her ten-year-old had brought home a note from school for disrupting the class, and her fourteen-year-old was having trouble with algebra. Sandy was sure that she was somehow the cause of their problems. To help her distinguish her responsibilities from her children's responsibilities, she made a list of what she could and could not control in the situation.

Sandy's List	
I Can Control	**I Cannot Control**
My choices (what I teach and give to my children)	Their choices (what they learn and receive)
My actions	Their actions or reactions
My thoughts and feelings	Their thoughts and feelings
Setting the rules and consequences	Their choice to obey or disobey

Result: Sandy felt relieved knowing she was not responsible for everything going on in her family. Rather than focusing on what she could not control—mainly her children's choices—she redirected her attention and energy to what she could control. She came up with a constructive plan for action benefiting herself and her children.

6. When you notice yourself thinking about something you cannot control.

> Ask yourself,
>
> *Do I really want to be thinking about this?*

If the answer is, "No," practice thinking about or doing something you can control.

Result: Your thinking becomes more objective and constructive, and you feel better.

If you have a habit of dwelling on the things in your life you cannot control, please see Central Principle 1: "Managing Your Thoughts," page 1.

PERSONAL APPLICATION

Prior to the big game, the players convinced themselves they were so good, they could not possibly lose. Although such thinking may seem positive, it is not realistic. No matter how good a team is, things over which they have no control can always occur that can cause defeat. A star player may become sick or injured, or the other team might play their all-time best.

Problem: When players do not consider the possibility of defeat (thus becoming overconfident), it is difficult for them to give their all during practice. If at any point in the game defeat seems possible, the players are not mentally prepared to face and overcome it or, if necessary, accept it gracefully.

Solution: Set a team goal and visualize success (devoting 10% of your time and energy here). Realistically acknowledge that winning or losing is the result of many factors, not all of which you have complete control over. Then focus energy on developing, practicing, and implementing a game plan (expending 90% of your time and energy here).

COMPETENCE WITHOUT CONFIDENCE

Whenever Kendall, an intelligent and capable speaker, prepared to speak at a business or church gathering, he thought a lot about whether the audience would react positively or negatively.

Problem: A lot of worry and anxiety.

Solution: Spend 10% of your time and energy considering the purpose or goal of your presentation—what you would like the audience to think, feel, or do as a result of your talk. Then give the bulk of your attention and energy (90%) to what you can control—your preparation and presentation.

MISGUIDED EFFORT

Gail believes that *if* she does what her husband Ralph wants (lose weight, be affectionate when he wants, and require little of him) *then* he will love her.

Problem: Gail assumes her actions (which she can control) will *cause* Ralph (whom she cannot control) to act in the way she wants. Although her actions have an influence on Ralph, how he chooses to respond to that influence is entirely up to him.

Solution: Gail decides she will contribute all she can (within reason) to the welfare of the marriage. She realizes, however, that unless Ralph does likewise, the marriage will be out of balance, causing additional problems and possible marital instability.

A GIFT WITH STRINGS ATTACHED

Sam gave his employees a substantial raise expecting to see a corresponding increase in productivity.

Problem: If the raise was given to produce or control future performance rather than reward past performance, the employee is apt to feel manipulated.

Consequence: The employee is apt to rebel, either passively or aggressively; and the employer is apt to feel an increase in anxiety or anger as he watches to see if the employee responds the way he *should*.

Solution: Sam gives the raise primarily as it was earned rather than an incentive for improved performance.

CONTROLLING RULES AND CONSEQUENCES, NOT CHILDREN

Cory and Cossette believe that IF they set a good example, teach correct principles, and discipline with love and firmness, *then* their children will behave properly.

Problem: When their children misbehave, Cory and Cossette are apt to feel responsible for their children's choices (which only the children, not the parents, can control).

Result: A vicious cycle can develop where children rebel against what feels to them like coercion, while parents keep trying harder *to make* the children obey.

Solution: Set a good example, teach correct principles, lovingly control rules and consequences (not the children), and allow for the fact that children will make their own choices and receive the consequences of their obedience or disobedience.

Result: When parents give their best in the areas *they* can control, children are most likely to choose to do their best in the areas *they* can control; sometimes, of course, children will choose to behave improperly, despite their parents best efforts.

Reminder: *If this central principle does not apply to your particular concern, go to another central principle OR go directly to the section on the problem you wish to solve: Communication Difficulties, Depression, Unsatisfactory Intimacy or Anxiety Attacks.*

RECOGNIZE YOUR INHERENT WORTH

Feelings of self-worth fluctuate throughout life, but your intrinsic worth and identity is a God-given fact that is secure and permanent. You have an inherent value independent of your feelings, your actions, or your accomplishments.

GENERAL INFORMATION

I do not know anyone who does not get down on himself occasionally. Everyone, regardless of age, intellect, accomplishment, position, or popularity, feels "I am not O.K.," or "I am not good enough" at times. These feelings come and go for all of us, regardless of our circumstances. *Feelings* of worth—as opposed to the *facts* of your inherent worth—are like the waves of the sea—continuously rising and falling. The only secure thing about the emotion of self-worth is that it is continuously in motion.

Self-worth is commonly thought of as something a person can get or lose. It is often measured by external things such as wealth, popularity, accomplishment, or others' opinions. For example, a person with great financial worth is often thought of as a worthwhile person. Nevertheless, money only measures wealth, not the things that really matter like happiness, love, intelligence, common sense, and family closeness. If internal worth is measured by external standards or fickle feelings over which you do not have complete control, your identity and your self-worth is built upon a shaky foundation.

BASIC PREMISE

Although the accomplishment of worthwhile things and a feeling of being worthwhile are highly desirable, I view self-worth more as a concrete fact than as an accomplishment or feeling. I believe each of us was born with a natural, spiritual, and biological predisposition to value ourselves as persons with inherent worth independent of success, failure, or the opinions of others.

Your inherent worth—as distinguished from the worth of your accomplishments and your worth to others—is like the pedigree or certificate of a thoroughbred horse. It is permanent and irrevocable. No opinion, feeling, or accomplishment can change your intrinsic identity and worth.

Somewhere inside of you is a natural sense of "I *am*" or identity. Permanently stamped or imprinted deeply in your mind is the certain knowledge that "I *am* me, a person of worth." Even when you make a mistake, experience failure, or feel worthless, your natural sense of self-worth says, "That's okay, just try again."

At birth you were given a name to identify who you are and to differentiate you from others. As a child with a natural sense of identity and worth—unless you were taught otherwise—there was no need to struggle with the age-old, philosophical question, "Who am I?" You knew who you were, even when you stumbled and fell.

For young children, usually less than eight years old, identity is not a question, it is a fact. Just ask a child,

"Who are you?" You will undoubtably hear, "I *am* Shannon" or "I *am* Melissa." You can ask the child to think of a time when he made a mistake or got into trouble, then ask him again, "Who are you?" The child will still tend to think in natural terms, "I *am* Shannon," rather than with the common adult tendency to add a negative label, such as, "I *am* stupid or not good enough."

Other than your name, you do not need a label to be special or unique. You are unique. Your particular combination of strengths, weaknesses, potential, and heritage is unlike anyone else's in the world—past, present, or future. Your identity is as exclusive as your fingerprints.

You—your inherent identity and worth—are like the hub of a wheel. The spokes may be thought of as the various characteristics, positions, relationships, and possessions you have. Although the spokes are important, they do not by themselves determine your identity or worth. See diagram on the next page

LOSING SIGHT OF NATURAL SELF-WORTH

Despite the biological stamp of inherent worth a child is born with, he receives new information from the environment. His personal identity is unintentionally labelled by the attitudes and actions of parents and other important and generally well-meaning adults. Good behavior usually results in "Good boy," while bad behavior brings forth a label of "Bad boy." Labelling a behavior or characteristic as good or bad may be appropriate, whereas using such a label on a person is inappropriate and can be harmful.

When a child is given a label affecting his identity or worth, he is faced with a dilemma. His natural instincts tell him he is a good, worthwhile person, independent of doing well or not. When he is labeled as a good and worthwhile person IF . . . and that he is not worthwhile unless . . . , what does he believe? His natural, pre-programmed beliefs or what others are saying? By the time a child is around eight years old, it is extremely likely

IDENTITY WHEEL

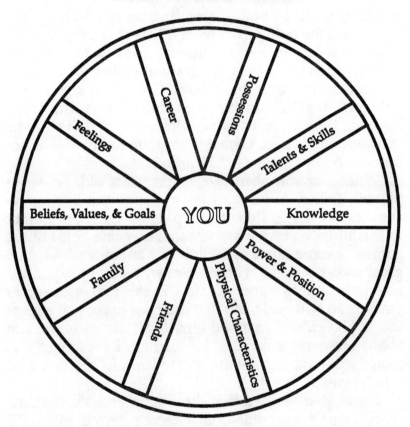

that a new tape or program will have developed in his mind, suggesting his self-worth depends largely on accomplishments and what others think.

Even in homes where caution is used in applying labels and in teaching a child the facts about who he is, a child still has a natural tendency to begin using personal labels of good or bad, depending on his accomplishments and the opinions of others. This proclivity for self-labeling, if left unchecked, can eat away at natural self-esteem much like weeds can gradually overrun a beautiful garden. Whether the natural, God-given tape or the subjective, artificial tape becomes the ruling force depends first on the child's environment and then, as he matures, on himself. Thus it is accurate to say, "I was not born with low self-esteem. I learned it."

When our son Shane was eight years old, he began playing soccer. Although I try not to sound like a psychologist at home, I could not pass up this opportunity to teach him an important lesson. After one of his initial games he came home and jubilantly announced, "I am a great soccer player." I asked him why and he explained how he scored two goals. I said, "Shane, that is great that you scored two goals, but that does not make you a great soccer player." I then asked him to tell me what was fun about the game and what he learned. I explained it is more important to have fun and to learn in sports than it is to be great.

I was glad we had that discussion because the next week Shane came home from a game dejected, saying, "I am a horrible soccer player." I again asked why. He explained he was playing goalie when he bent over to stop the ball and it rolled between his legs scoring the goal that lost the game for his team. I said, "Shane, you made a mistake, but that does not make you a terrible soccer player. Now, did you have some fun during your game? And, what did you learn?" He got the point.

Although this principle is so simple that a child can understand it, an adult often shakes his head in utter confusion. When you ask an adult, "Who are you?" there tends to be a long pause after which you are apt to hear a variety of labels: I am an attorney, a housewife, an engineer or I am fat, bright, rich, lazy, or popular. This common way of thinking leads a person to base his intrinsic worth on variables (possessions, accomplishments, or the opinions of others) that can be taken away or lose their value, rather than on the natural and secure fact that "I AM," therefore, "I have worth and value."

YOU ARE NOT YOUR ROLES

Although everyone has important roles to fulfill (son, daughter, brother, sister, father, mother, husband, wife, friend, employer, employee, athlete, musician), you are NOT your roles. You are more than your career, you are more than your body, you are more than your marriage, and you are more than your accomplishments or lack of accomplishments. You are more than any of these things. This simple truth is obvious when we stop to think about it; nevertheless, many people define their identity by what they do.

You can think of your various roles in life as hats you wear: the hats are yours, but you are more than your hats. Your roles describe your responsibilities and to some extent, what you do; however they do not completely describe you (your strengths, weaknesses, potential, and personality).

BASING SELF-WORTH ON FEELING WORTHWHILE

Wanting to feel good about yourself is natural, but since feelings are fickle and emotion is constantly in motion, basing your identity or worth on how you feel is inherently unstable and insecure. If you base your self-worth on feelings, your view of your self-worth is on an emotional roller coaster ride and you feel less secure.

If you forget about the rock solid foundation you were born with and instead base your sense of worth on how you feel, your life is like a house built upon a sandy foundation. As long as things are going well, you tend to feel worthwhile. But when the clear weather passes and the storms of life come (illness, loss of job, loss of loved ones) your very worth as a person will seem to hang in a precarious state. Even amidst the good times, just knowing you could lose "everything" can interfere with fully enjoying your successes. The result is an increased sense of stress and anxiety.

Building self-esteem on feelings or possessions is like the man in the Bible who built his house on sand. The rains came and the house fell. But the man who built his house on rock—on a firm foundation—saw his house endure. Feelings and possessions may pass, but your own God-given uniqueness, abilities, and potential will endure.

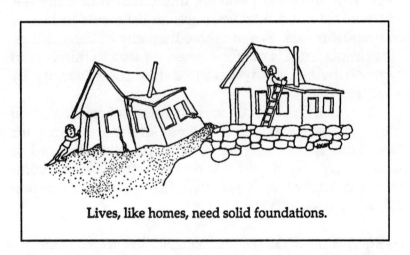

Lives, like homes, need solid foundations.

STEPS TO APPLYING THE PRINCIPLE

The steps for applying the principle are divided into three sections:

1. Avoid seeking after what you already have.

2. Look at yourself objectively.

3. Accept your natural self-worth.

AVOID SEEKING WHAT YOU ALREADY HAVE

1. Beware of "Identity Questions" such as, Who am I?" or "Am I worthwhile?" The fact is, you are worthwhile. So do not keep asking a never-ending question such as, "Who am I?" or "Am I worthwhile?" Repeatedly asking such questions is depressing. Instead, ask questions that lead to constructive action, such as, "What shall I do that is worthwhile?"

2. Notice if you set up tests to determine your worth. For example, "I am worthwhile if I get a promotion," "I am lovable if he loves me," "I am intelligent if I communicate well." Testing your self-worth is self-defeating. You cannot win.

   Even if you score high on several tests, you never know how you will do next time. The threat of not being worthwhile lurks around every corner. Continually questioning your self-worth leads to never-ending tests and increasing self-doubt.

   Trying to find self-worth reminds me of the time I looked all over the house, from top to bottom, for my glasses, only to discover I was wearing them all along.

3. Trying to secure feelings of self-worth is a losing battle, because emotion is constantly in motion. You do not need to fight for something you already have.

   Take off the emotional battle fatigues and peacefully do things you consider worthwhile, regardless of how you feel. The worst that could happen is that you will feel badly about yourself while doing good things. It is much more likely, though, that your feelings of self-worth will continue to fluctuate, but without the extreme highs and lows.

4. Strive to minimize or, if possible eliminate, comparisons of yourself to others. Comparing leads to lower self-esteem or artificially inflated self-esteem.

   Key point: Most comparisons are exaggerated and extremely inaccurate because people tend to compare their insides with others' outsides or they compare their weaknesses with others' strengths.

5. If your goal is to be someone or to be worthwhile, the underlying assumption may be, I am not someone or I am not worthwhile. It is better to think and talk in terms of what you want to do, rather than what you want TO BE.

   Example: "I want to work at the Bank of America and someday manage the local branch, rather than I want TO BE a banker."

LOOK AT YOURSELF OBJECTIVELY

1. Observe how you use the two most important words affecting your identity and self-esteem—I am.

   Caution: Any habitual use of these words to describe yourself in any other way than, for example, "I am Laurie," "I am a person," "I am a child of God," "I am a woman" may be hazardous to your self-esteem.

> *Key Point:* Avoid using good or bad labels to identify yourself or others ("I am smart" or "I am dumb").

2. Likewise, observe how you use the two most important words affecting your view of others—"He is . . ." or "You are . . ."

   Caution: Any habitual use of these words to describe others in any other way than, "He is Roger," "He is a person," "He is a child of God," "He is a man" may be detrimental to your relationships and your self-esteem.

3. Rather than attempting to describe who you are, describe what you think, feel, do, or have.

   Example: I have certain talents, accomplishments, and relationships. Or I like to play the piano, jog, and spend time with friends.

4. For additional practice distinguishing who you are from what you have:

   Take a piece of paper and draw a vertical line down the center. On the top of the left side, write "I AM," and on the top of the right side, write "I HAVE."

   List as many things about yourself as you can, placing them on the appropriate side of the line. Remember, only put factual, permanent, rock-solid statements about yourself in the "I AM" column. See the example on the following page.

ACCEPT YOUR NATURAL SELF-WORTH

1. If you are concerned that your productivity or motivation will diminish by accepting your natural self-worth, consider the following:

I Am versus I Have

I Am	I Have
Me	Thoughts (good and bad)
John	
A Child of God	Feelings (pleasant and unpleasant)
A Person with Strengths, Weaknesses, and Potential	Habits (good and bad)
	Accomplishments (successes and failures)
Male	
	Possessions
	Family relationships

Myth: If I accept the notion I am worthwhile, perhaps I will become lazy and fail to accomplish some important things.

Fact: Everyone has a natural desire to improve and accomplish, though some have learned to ignore it. When you strive to achieve something because of its value to you rather than because you are attempting to achieve self-worth, you are more likely to enjoy your successes and more successfully survive your failures.

Myth: If I accept the belief I have natural worth, then I am no different from anyone else.

Fact: You have a particular combination of strengths, weaknesses and potential as unique as your fingerprints. You are special.

2. Decide that you want to accept what you were born knowing: that you have inherent worth, independent of others' opinions or anything you do. Then you can strengthen or regain your childhood faith in yourself.

- Answer the question of "Am I worthwhile?" once and for all. Take several 3x5 cards and write the following words or something similar:

> "I am worthwhile because I am me, a child of God with a unique blend of strengths, weaknesses, and potential."

- Place the cards where you can see them at least a dozen times a day (refrigerator, T.V., mirror, or the visor of your automobile).

- Use your feelings as a trigger to remind you of what you wrote on your cards. Whenever you feel depressed or doubt your self-worth, say to yourself, "I am worthwhile because I AM me, a child of God with a unique blend of strengths, weaknesses, and potential." By doing this you are using feelings of self-doubt to help remember what you once knew so naturally.

- To further reinforce your effort to build a solid foundation, share what you are working on with someone.

3. Notice that your efforts to prove you are worthwhile are never quite enough. Just as you cannot prove the existence of God, you cannot prove you are worthwhile, no matter how hard you try.

   Key Point: Although you cannot prove you are worthwhile, you can choose to believe in your worth as a person; you can develop faith in yourself.

Definition of faith: To hope for things which are not seen or provable but which are nevertheless true.

4. Even though you were born with a sense of your inherent worth, it is easy to forget that you truly are worthwhile. Like the tiny, proverbial mustard seed (Matthew 13:31; Alma 32), your natural faith in yourself is easy to overlook. Fortunately, however, it is never too late to nurture that seed.

5. Consider developing faith in your inherent worth just as you have in other aspects of your life such as the faith you have in your ability to graduate from school, do a job, learn a skill, or play a sport.

6. Nurture your natural inclination—your seed of faith—to believe in yourself.

   • Give your self-worth the benefit of the doubt. Exercise a particle of faith, even if you can no more than desire to believe that you have your own unique worth as a person. Allow yourself to hope it is true—that you truly are worthwhile.

   • Listen to those around you who know the truth about your worth (loved ones, friends, and trusted associates). Ask those who care about you whether or not they believe you have any worth.

- Even though you may not feel worthwhile, give yourself permission to believe others when they say you have worth.

Strengthen your faith in your inherent worth by doing things you consider worthwhile.

Caution: If you do worthwhile things in an attempt to prove you are worthwhile or that you are not worthless, you will fail. On the other hand, if you believe you are worthwhile yet neglect doing worthwhile things, your natural faith in yourself will diminish.

Key Point: Striving to do worthwhile things is essential to your success and happiness, but it is NOT the foundation of your self-worth.

Example: Sharon doubts her worth unless she does everything right. Bill, on the other hand, believes he is worthwhile because he does so many things right. It would be better if Sharon and Bill each recognize they have inherent worth, independent of how well they do things.

Be patient. Faith in yourself, like a mustard seed grows slowly; nevertheless, it will in time become a strong tree and bear good fruit.

7. Frequently reassure yourself that feelings of low self-esteem or worthlessness, though normal, do not change the fact of your God-given worth.

Remember: Your fundamental identity and worth is a fact, not a feeling.

PERSONAL APPLICATION

I spent several weeks trying to help Cari overcome a lifelong feeling of worthlessness. I asked her to tell me if others viewed her similarly to the way she viewed herself. "Oh, I don't believe so," she said. Others viewed her as a loving wife and mother. Her manager at the bank viewed her as dedicated and hard working. At church and in the community, she was known as someone who was willing to help and serve others.

Although she was aware of the good things she did and of others' love and appreciation, she continued to feel badly about herself. I reasoned and reasoned with her. Sometimes she argued persuasively that she just was not good enough. Other times she acknowledged that my reasoning seemed valid; nevertheless, she could not accept the idea that she had unchangeable worth.

Because she forgot what she once naturally knew as a child—that she has inherent, God-given worth—she repeatedly asked, "Am I worthwhile?" The more she asked the question, the more she doubted herself. She was caught in a vicious cycle, a never ending test of her worth as a person. No matter how much she accomplished, how often others praised her, or how good she felt about herself, she kept asking the same question. Having lost her childhood faith in herself, she could not simply answer, "Yes, I am worthwhile."

The problem in Cari's case was not so much a lack of effort, accomplishment, or actual worth, but having forgotten what she once knew so well as a child thenshe developed the self-defeating habit of questioning and doubting her instinctive or God-given sense of worth. Repeatedly asking herself, "Am I worthwhile?" became as much a problem as forgetting the answer.

Since the answer was preprogrammed in her mind, I knew once she stopped consciously and repetitively asking whether or not she was worthwhile, the natural answer would begin to emerge. I suggested she *stop* asking the question. She agreed. Instead, she simply went about doing her usual things. Whenever the question popped into her mind, she dismissed it and went about doing her business.

As she thought less about the question, an interesting thing happened—she became less troubled about her identity and worth. It was not so much that she suddenly felt great about herself—who does?—but she no longer doubted her worth as a person.

Example—A Shaky Foundation of Self-worth

Fred had no doubt about his worth. He was the greatest. He was the president and owner of a large corporation. He was a popular and influential member of his community. He had plenty of money, a big house, and expensive cars. He was also an exceptionally talented and successful athlete.

One night Fred failed in bed with his wife, whom he loved dearly. The next night he tried harder, but to no avail. With each succeeding effort—and failure—he became increasingly discouraged and down on himself and eventually concluded, "I *am* a failure."

Fred had spent a lifetime convincing himself he was worthwhile *because* of his performance in school, athletics, business, community, and everything else he did. When he experienced failure, he naturally, though mistakenly, believed *he* was a failure. Before he could resolve his problem, it was necessary for him rediscover that his worth as a person was intrinsic, not based primarily on his performance. *Result:* When he realized he was worthwhile—even lovable—independent of his impressive list of successes, as well as his recent failures, he not only felt better, but to his delight, performed better.

Reminder: *If this central principle does not apply to your particular concern, go to another central principle OR go directly to the section on the problem you wish to solve: Communication Difficulties, Depression, Unsatisfactory Intimacy, or Anxiety Attacks.*

BUILD A FIRM FOUNDATION FOR YOUR PERSONAL SECURITY

Your security in life depends more on how you manage yourself than on any other person or thing.

GENERAL INFORMATION

Although some things are more secure than others, nothing in this world is entirely secure. There are some things, of course, you have more control over than others; nevertheless, any relationship or thing in this world can be lost or taken away, despite your best efforts. Except for things pertaining to the Lord—who is unchangeable—everything else has some degree of insecurity associated with it.

Of course, the better you manage yourself, the more personal security you will have. As you develop more knowledge and skill, you are better equipped to deal with the opportunities and difficulties of life, whatever they may be. As you gain greater control over yourself, learning to live in a well-balanced, reasonable, and virtuous manner, you have a greater degree of security. For example, if you take good care of your body, your health is more secure. If you spend quality time with your family, your home life is more secure; and if you manage your money well, you are more financially secure. Note that I said you are *more* secure, *not completely* secure.

FEELINGS OF SECURITY FLUCTUATE NO MATTER HOW SECURE YOU ARE

Regardless of the degree of security you obtain in this life, your feelings of security or insecurity still fluctuate. Even people who manage themselves well feel self-doubts and insecurities from time to time. Though the intensity and degree of those feelings is usually less, they still exist. For example, Abraham Lincoln, one of our greatest presidents, experienced periods of deep depression; even Moses, with his outstanding spiritual and leadership qualities, felt woefully inadequate at times.

THE IRONY ABOUT TRYING TO FEEL SECURE

There is an interesting irony about trying to obtain the elusive and imaginary goal of emotional security. Even though the goal may *seem* reasonable, the fact is, you cannot attain it. The goal itself contributes to feeling less secure. Usually, the harder you try the worse you feel. On the other hand, when you put more effort into improving yourself and your relationships with others, you usually end up feeling *better*.

Many clients come to my office with the goal of feeling secure or eliminating feelings of insecurity. Occasionally I tell them if they find a way to secure feelings of security, let me know. We will sell it and make billions. Except for those in the tobacco, alcohol, and drug industry—who sell artificially induced feelings of security—everyone else will be delighted.

> *Key point:* The goal to feel secure or to eliminate
> feelings of insecurity is futile. It is like trying
> to control the waves at the beach.

THE MORE SURE FOUNDATION FOR
YOUR SECURITY—YOU

Your personal security is better thought of in terms of what you can control (mainly yourself), rather than on what you cannot completely control (what others' think of you, how nice a house or car you have, or how secure you feel). Although you cannot control all the circumstances in your life, you can learn to control yourself. As you do, you become *more* secure.

At the very core of what you control is what you think. Regardless of your circumstances, you can choose what you think and what you value. Not even torture and inhumane treatment in P.O.W. concentration camps, for example, can take away a soldier's love of God, family, and freedom. Within any given situation and the choices available in that situation, you are free to choose what you will think and do. No one can take away your freedom to choose. Likewise, no one can stop you from strengthening your foundation for security as you learn to better manage yourself and your relationship with others. But remember, even with a reasonably secure foundation, your feelings of security will still fluctuate to some extent.

BASING YOUR SECURITY ON YOURSELF—
A NATURAL TENDENCY

The natural tendency to base your security primarily on yourself rather than on others is seen in a child's instinctive drive to become increasingly self-reliant (learning to crawl, then walk, run, ride a bike, then drive a car). Although the child allows others to teach and help him, he ultimately wants to do things on his own. How often have you heard a child say, "I want to do it myself!" Even a child with a beloved security blanket eventually leaves it behind—sometimes however, only after a loving parent removes it. Then, as the child continues to learn and mature, he becomes more independent

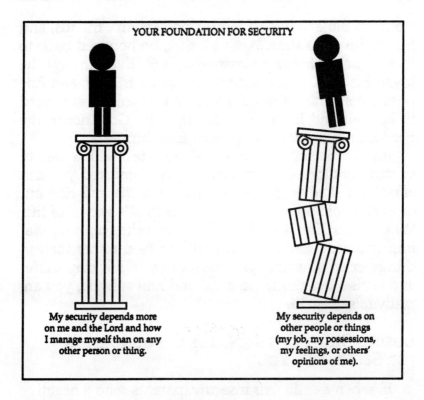

YOUR FOUNDATION FOR SECURITY

My security depends more
on me and the Lord and how
I manage myself than on any
other person or thing.

My security depends on
other people or things
(my job, my possessions,
my feelings, or others'
opinions of me).

and secure, even though feelings of security fluctuate along the way.

If, when a child feels the normal, periodic feelings of insecurity, he is given reassurance that he is still all right, worthwhile, and capable, he generally learns to ride out the waves of emotion without giving them much thought or attention. He knows those feelings of insecurity will pass, so he focuses his attention and effort on doing things he considers important *despite* feeling insecure for awhile.

THE BENEFITS

A person with a well developed degree of personal security can lose a loved one, a job, his wealth, or even his health, and still have the ability and stability to regroup and effectively proceed with life. Consider Job, from the Bible, who lost family, possessions, friends, and his health for a time. After all that, he bounced back to live a successful and prosperous life. Even though he loved his family and valued his health, friends, and fine possessions, his personal security was solidly anchored in himself and in his relationship with God, not in the people or things that were taken from him.

Just as the skilled surfer is able to deal with a variety of surf conditions, when you are well-prepared you can effectively deal with the vicissitudes of life and ride out or even avoid some of the more traumatic waves of life. When your life is anchored in self-reliance, personal improvement, and an active faith in God rather than in things or in other people, the storms of life may buffet and bruise, but when the wind and rain subside, you are ready to sail again.

LOSING SIGHT OF THE NATURAL FOUNDATION FOR SECURITY—YOU

If, when a child *feels* insecure, parents send a negative message ("You are not good enough," "You are upsetting us," or "You should not feel that way") the child will likely experience more pain or difficulty than he knows how to handle. Then, rather than continuing on the natural course of basing his security on himself, he tends to get sidetracked, looking outside of himself for comfort and security.

Avoiding or minimizing pain then becomes the main goal instead of improving himself and accomplishing worthwhile things. Rather than doing the kind of things that lead to greater personal security, the child is likely to seek after alluring, counterfeit forms of security that promise feeling good once and for all, but always fail. He may, for example, become obsessed with being better than others in order to alleviate his suffering and insecurity; he may shy away from social or competitive activities out of fear of not being good enough; or he may attempt to anesthetize his pain with alcohol, drugs, or sex.

If the child does excel—in part because he is attempting to alleviate feelings of insecurity—he may become irrationally driven to maintain or achieve a yet higher level of success that makes a balanced, happy life difficult. I see this type of obsessive drive in some people who have achieved high levels of business or social success.

Or if "success" eludes this type person or becomes too difficult to obtain, he may give up or find some other way to escape how he *feels* about himself through alcohol, drugs, sex, or even T.V. Instead of simply focusing on developing and using skills that lead to a well-balanced and relatively secure life, he rides a treacherous treadmill seeking a fixed and secure *feeling*.

STEPS TO APPLY THE PRINCIPLE

1. Think of a time in your life when you were particularly independent and self-reliant. Write a brief description of a poignant event during that time. For the next month, review and try to relive that event for a few minutes, three times a day.

   Example: Sally inadvertently became dependent on her husband, much to his dismay. She could hardly make a decision without worrying about whether or not he would approve. At first she could not think of a time when she was more independent and self-reliant, even though this had not become her pattern until after she was married. Finally, she thought back to a time in college when she was living with a roommate. Although she was considerate of her companion, she recalled how she made decisions independently, based on what she thought was best. I asked her to recall those times three times a day, possibly before each meal. As Sally did this, she began to rediscover her ability to think and act independently.

2. Monitor the amount of attention you place on doing things that make you more secure (such as improving yourself, your skills, your relationships with others and with the Lord) versus the attention you place on trying to find security in the things of the world (the praise or acceptance of others, more money and possessions, or a gorgeous body).

3. Remind yourself that the goal to find security through other people or things tends to produce greater insecurity. By increasing your awareness of what you are basing your security on, your mind will tend to gravitate toward the natural instinct of developing a solid personal foundation.

4. Strengthen your personal security by improving yourself physically, mentally, socially, professionally, and spiritually. Set a goal, make a plan—work on it. As you do you will become increasingly secure and the inevitable feelings of insecurity will become less intense and less frequent.

5. If you tend to base your personal security on someone or something other than yourself:

   • Take several 3x5 cards and write something like:

   > *"My happiness and security depends more on me and the Lord and how well I manage myself than on any other person or thing."*

- Place the cards where you can see them at least a dozen times a day (on the refrigerator, T.V., mirror, or the visor of your automobile).

- Use your feelings of insecurity as a trigger to remind you of what you have written on your cards. Each time you feel insecure, say to yourself: "My happiness and security depends more on me and the Lord, and how well I manage myself than on any other person or thing."

Result: Your insecurities will actually help you become more secure.

- To further reinforce them in your mind, share your efforts and improvements with someone else.

PERSONAL APPLICATION

As a teenager who often felt insecure, Mark frequently envisioned himself feeling secure and worthwhile when he would someday be a multimillionaire. It was not so much the money that he wanted, but the feelings of security that so easily alluded him as a youth.

For the next twenty years or so he studied and worked hard, often harder than anyone around him. To those who knew Mark, he was dedicated or driven to be the best employee or manager he could possibly be. That certainly was true, but even more important to Mark, and unknown to others, was his underlying quest for security.

Mark was thirty-eight years old when he sold the company he started, for three million dollars—cash. His dream came true. He spent the next year buying everything he wanted and traveling around the world.

During his first appointment he told me his story. I was impressed with his accomplishments, not to mention the exotic Lamborgini parked in front of my office. He then dropped the bombshell—he did not feel any more secure now than he did before. In spite of all that hard work, a successful company, and a great deal of money, he still felt insecure. His lifelong plan for personal security failed. He was depressed—extremely depressed.

He did not know what to do with his life now. He still wanted to feel secure, but he had absolutely no idea of how to go about it. He knew he could start another company and perhaps succeed again, but he also knew that would not make him feel secure.

Although Mark came to understand that success and wealth does not, in and of itself, bring security, he was not ready to look at himself. He was afraid he could not stand the pain of facing up to being as insecure and inadequate as he perceived himself to be. His life and his perspective were so out of balance he was now, more than ever, convinced he was a failure. Unfortunately, he did not return after that first visit. Still, he provided a vivid example to me of the futility of building our lives on externals.

Rebuilding a Solid Foundation for Personal Security

As a child, Gloria was emotionally abused. To escape her pain she dreamed of the day when a man would love her so much she would feel secure in his arms. During college she found such a man. Tom was a confident, take-charge person. He was also very demanding, but Gloria did not mind. She bent over backwards to please him, because she loved him and because she *needed* his love in order to feel secure.

What she did not realize was that underneath his strong exterior, he felt just as insecure as she felt. His way to battle feelings of insecurity was to appear calm, strong, and rational. He needed to be in control. They both became dependent on one another—or codependent.

Before I helped Gloria rebuild her foundation for security, I explained what would probably happen in the marriage as she became stronger and more self-reliant, rather than Tom-reliant. At first, she had trouble imagining Tom feeling insecure at all, let alone being somewhat dependent on her. But then she began to recall that when she would start to do things for herself such as taking a class, spending time with her friends, or expressing a different opinion, Tom would become irritable and accuse her of being selfish and inconsiderate of his feelings. She began to realize his agitation was not her fault, but rather an indication he was basing his security on her and on her being dependent on him.

They were stuck, like two crabs in a bucket. Neither one could get out because the other one would not allow it. As soon as one climbed near the top, the other pulled him back down. Neither one could stand being alone, although they did not get along very well together.

Even though Gloria now realized that becoming stronger would be as hard on Tom as on her, she decided to do it, not to control him but because she loved him dearly and wanted their marriage to succeed. Tom refused to see me at first because, of course, he believed Gloria was the one with the problem. Nevertheless, Gloria began making some constructive changes in her thinking and behavior. Despite regularly reassuring Bill she loved him, Tom became increasingly agitated, especially as she learned to say "No" in a firm and polite way.

Eventually Tom realized that Gloria was becoming stronger and happier and he was feeling worse and was even worried he might lose her. Tom came to see me, but unlike Mark in the previous example, was brave enough to look at himself and admit his foundation for personal security had a crack in it. He humbly recognized his dependency on being in control and having Gloria *need* him.

It was uncomfortable for Tom and Gloria to initially untangle their codependency and establish two separate and independent foundations. With a great deal of courage—and encouragement—they not only became self-reliant, but they committed themselves to building a loving and respectful marriage. They are now like two independent, yet connected pillars, supporting the marital bridge they *both* designed and built.

> **Reminder:** *If this central principle does not apply to your particular concern, go to another central principle OR go directly to the section on the problem you wish to solve: Communication Difficulties, Depression, Unsatisfactory Intimacy, or Anxiety Attacks.*

PRINCIPLE 7

SET YOUR MINIMUM STANDARDS

In any situation or relationship there are minimum requirements or standards you consider necessary for it to be acceptable (quite different from ideal or perfect.) While still striving to obtain the ideal, define your minimum standards. Measure quality or performance as being above or below your minimum acceptable standard.

GENERAL INFORMATION

Just as you have some idea of what perfection is in most any situation or relationship, there is also some level of performance you consider acceptable and satisfactory, even though it is less than ideal. Although you naturally strive to obtain what you consider ideal, you can know you are doing a good job when you at least measure up to your minimum standards of performance.

The idea of distinguishing minimum standards from an ideal is not new. There are examples all around us. To be admitted to a university, for example, one must meet academic requirements that are essential and non-negotiable though usually less than the ideal of straight A's. To obtain a driver license, one need not be a perfect driver although there are specific requirements that must be met.

Knowing in advance what the prerequisites are lets you know where you stand and what your choices are. If you do not currently qualify, for instance, you can generally do something about it. Fortunately, even though you are not perfect, you can objectively and confidently know when you do measure up to the minimum requirements or what to do when you do not.

Some people, however, worry that identifying and focusing on a minimum acceptable standard will drive them or a relationship toward mediocrity. They are afraid of losing sight of the long term goal of excellence or perfection. To the contrary, as long as you have a clear goal or vision, defining a minimum standard gives you a baseline or benchmark to make sure you are first maintaining, and then exceeding, as you strive toward your goal.

REASONS FOR SETTING A MINIMUM STANDARD

Everyone wants to succeed in life, to measure up. Often the definition of success, however, involves obtaining a seemingly impossible ideal relationship, position, or performance (a family like Ozzie and Harriet, a perfectly neat and clean house, being the president of a company, or having a picture perfect body).

Striving for perfection is desirable, but what happens when you measure your performance against a standard of perfection. How can you ever feel that your present level is acceptable? If you ever do obtain that which you consider to be ideal, the odds are you will simply raise the level of what you consider ideal. You never measure up. No matter how hard you try or how well you do, it is not good enough—at least as measured against the ideal of perfection.

Result: Continuously assessing your performance as inadequate is upsetting and discouraging and drains valuable energy that could better be used in productive pursuits.

Being totally satisfied with a minimally acceptable job, on the other hand, without striving toward an ideal can interfere with your progress and lead to personal stagnation. Without an ideal to strive toward, you will not be at your best. That is why successful businesses and individuals develop mission statements, core values, and goals to strive toward, knowing full well that daily performance will be somewhat less than the ideal.

You Have the Right to Set Your Own Standards

It is your right to determine the minimum requirements or standards you consider necessary for a relationship or personal performance to be acceptable. You can set your standards at whatever level you like; it is up to you. You could, for instance, unreasonably decide that anything less than a perfect spouse is unacceptable. Or, at the other extreme, you could decide anyone who breathes and is willing to marry you qualifies.

You Do Not Have the Right to Force Others to Live Up to Your Standards

Although your standards may define your requirements for another person's performance (in a marital, business, or social relationship), you do *not*, however, have the right to force someone to accept or live up to your standard. That is their choice. Nor does having the right to set your standards mean you are necessarily right.

Key point: The word standard or requirement refers to what you consider necessary for a performance or relationship to be acceptable to you; it does NOT mean you have the right to force someone to accept or live up to your requirements.

THREE BENEFITS OF DEFINING YOUR MINIMUM STANDARDS

First: Rather than comparing yourself to some ideal—and constantly failing—you have a practical and objective benchmark from which to measure your performance. You can then measure your performance as being at, below, or above your standard. No doubt you will feel encouraged in some areas where you are at or above standard, while in other areas you will see the need for improvement. It is refreshing to be able to feel good at some level of performance (in marriage, at work, at home, or in personal activities) while still striving for a higher level. You will also find yourself having more control over evaluating your success, since you can rely more on your own criteria and judgement than on what others think.

Second: When your minimum standards are clear to you and you are adhering to them, you send a clear signal, often unspoken, to others of what you require of them and of yourself. When others know where your line is—that which distinguishes the things you are willing to negotiate from the things you are unwilling to negotiate— they are generally more comfortable—if not at first, at least later. They know where they stand with you. Then they can more securely examine the available choices in the relationship because you have drawn a line. For instance, if honesty is one of your minimum standards, others will know there is no point in arguing or trying to manipulate you into doing something dishonest.

Of course, if someone finds your standards or requirements unacceptable, they do not have to adhere to them. The relationship, however, will be off balance and unlikely to progress until each other's minimum standards are mutually acceptable.

Third: You have an objective criteria to evaluate where someone else stands relative to your standards. In marriage, for instance, if you consider respect an essential, non-negotiable ingredient, you are able to accurately assess your spouse's behavior in that area. If there is a problem, you can clearly communicate and focus on it until a solution is found, even if it takes weeks or months.

In every healthy relationship, whether personal or business, minimum standards are mutually understood and respected. The process of identifying the basic rules or requirements for the relationship often occurs naturally. If you are in a relationship where things are going well, you may not need to formally identify and discuss your minimum standards.

The idea of minimum standards is depicted in the diagram on the following page.

STEPS TO APPLYING THE PRINCIPLE

First, general steps for applying this principle are given. These steps apply in any situation. Additional steps are suggested for application in four special situations:

1) In a relationship between peers (premarital or marital)

2) In a relationship with non-peers (grandparents, parents, or children)

An Ideal Goal or State of Perfection

Strive to Achieve the Ideal

In marriage, for example, you might strive for a peaceful, happy, loving relationship.

In addition to ideals that are mutually agreed upon, many of the things above this line are preferences that are negotiable (love of music or sports, hair color, or height). Shelly, my wife, always wanted a husband who could dance. Fortunately for me, that was not one of her minimum requirements for a marriage partner.

The things you place below this line are non-negotiable.

My Minimum Standards for an Acceptable Relationship

In marriage, your minimum standards might include:

1) Respect: We value each others' opinions and feelings, even when there are differences; there will be no name calling or yelling.

2) Commitment: Our relationship is more important than any other mortal relationship, including relationships with children, extended family, friends, or business associates.

3) Fidelity: We will not engage in intimate involvement with members of the opposite sex.

4) Good communication: We speak to each other kindly and honestly. We solve problems in a constructive way, where we both benefit.

5) Self-reliance: Each of us stands independently of the other. We can think rationally and act responsibly, without requiring the others' permission or approval.

6) Friendship. We are each other's best friend.

Evaluate the relationship as being at, below, or above your standard.

3) In a relationship where one person has authority over the other (in business, civic, or church organizations)

4) In private or personal activities (exercise, diet, neatness, car care, and so forth)

GENERAL STEPS

1. Make a list of things you consider necessary and non-negotiable (your minimum standards) for a relationship, performance, or situation to be acceptable.

   Note: Although you could come up with something unreasonable, it is extremely unlikely. I have gone through this exercise with hundreds of people with less than a handful even listing one unreasonable requirement.

   Reason: This is not a wish list. You are making a clear distinction between your ideal preferences and your minimum requirements.

2. After you complete your list, go back and add specific examples for each thing on your list. When you have general items on your list, such as "Respect," make sure you provide specific, behavioral examples that allow you and your companion to objectively determine whether that standard is being adhered to or not.

   Example: Respect means to me, no yelling or name calling. It means we acknowledge each other's right to differing opinions and feelings. Words like, 'I understand' or 'I see we have a different perspective on this, and that's okay' are frequently heard.

3. If possible, have another person—one who is objective—review your list of minimum standards. His reaction and comments can help you evaluate the reasonableness of your standards, and also suggest some ways to add to or refine the items on your list.

4. Use your minimum standards as a criteria to measure quality or performance, while continuing to strive to achieve your ideal.

ADDITIONAL STEPS

In a relationship between peers (pre-marital, marital, friendships):

1. Before sharing your minimum standards with your companion, invite him to make a list of his own minimum standards. Unless he is given an opportunity to clarify his standards before you share yours, he is apt to feel overwhelmed or pressured.

   A common concern many voice is, "I do not have the right to set standards for how someone else acts." The answer to this is that you are defining standards for a relationship that is acceptable to you. Whether someone else agrees or not is up to them.

2. While reading each other's minimum standards, look first for things you both share. Next, look at things that at first glance seem to conflict.

   Caution: Make sure you understand each other's standards before you attempt to resolve any differences.

3. If you do not understand what is meant by a certain thing, ask questions ("What do you mean by . . . ," or, "Could you give me an example of . . . ?").

4. In reconciling discrepancies between each others' standards, seek to find ways to honor each others standards without violating your own.

   Key point: When discussing discrepancies show respect for your companion's opinions, feelings, and standards, while seeking a mutually satisfactory solution.

5. If, however, you are unable to find a way to honor each others' standards without violating your own integrity—especially in a marriage—I encourage you to seek professional help. See Appendix, "How To Select A Therapist."

In a Relationship With Non-Peers

1. After you write your minimum standards, including specific examples, kindly announce your position.

   Key point: This is not a discussion or debate, but a declaration or announcement of the standards by which you live in a particular relationship. There is no need to defend, justify, or excuse the standards you set or the line you draw. The following three steps are helpful in making your announcement.

   - State your love and appreciation for the person.
   - Share your minimum standards.
   - Share your hopes for the relationship.

2. Sharing your standards in a letter can be helpful.

   Result: You give the other person a chance to privately read and think about what you said, thereby increasing the likelihood of him understanding that you are doing this for the mutual benefit of the relationship rather than trying to control him. A letter is especially helpful if the other person is apt to initially misinterpret or overreact.

IN A RELATIONSHIP WHERE ONE PERSON HAS AUTHORITY OVER THE OTHER

Note: When you are reporting to someone with authority over you, it is usually necessary to obtain their approval. In essence, you are writing your own job description. You are defining the standards by which your performance will be measured by you and your boss.

1. After you have written your minimum standards, schedule a time to meet with the person to whom you report. Preface your presentation by explaining you wish to do the best possible job and would like him to review some standards of performance you came up with. In my experience it is rare for someone to set their standards too low. It is more likely for them to be too high, too idealistic, such that the boss's feedback suggests a lesser, more realistic standard. When you and he agree on your standards, you have an objective, reasonable criteria to measure and evaluate your performance.

   Result: You can objectively evaluate your own job performance, without having to anxiously await someone else's evaluation.

2. Strive to meet, maintain, and then exceed your minimum standards.

3. As your skills increase, you may wish to raise your minimum standards (and, in some cases, your ideals as well).

In Private, Personal Activities

1. Make a list of that which you consider necessary for your performance to be acceptable to you (not to anyone else). Be specific.

Example: At five feet 10 inches, I consider my weight acceptable as long as it is between 168 and 172 pounds, with 165 pounds ideal. I also exercise a minimum of 3 times a week, 4 to 5 times ideally. As long as my weight is between 168 and 172 pounds and I exercise at least 3 times a week, I am pleased; when I do better, I am delighted.

Example: My wife, Shelly, would ideally like the house immaculate, but with five children and a husband, that ideal is usually unobtainable. If she thought of the ideal as her minimum standard, she would be frustrated much of the time. Instead, she has minimum standards of order and cleanliness she considers acceptable, though not ideal (beds made in the morning, kitchen cleaned after each meal, and house picked up before dinner).

PERSONAL APPLICATION

As I was growing up I knew precisely what kind of marriage I did not want to have. Even so, I was afraid I would become emotionally involved with someone, get married, and then wake up some morning realizing I made a mistake. I did not trust my feelings, by themselves, to help me make a wise decision on who to marry.

To make matters worse, I also realized that dwelling on what I was afraid of would keep those things prominent in my mind, thereby increasing the likelihood of getting trapped in the very thing I was determined to avoid. I did some private research to find out what a good marriage—at least for me—would be like. I observed lots of marriages. I even watched "Leave It to Beaver."

MAKING A LIST

I began to develop a mental list of characteristics I felt were necessary for me to have a good marriage. What I came up with was not the typical, pie-in-the-sky, marital wish list. They were the rock-bottom necessary ingredients, the things I would not compromise on. They were the non-negotiables, my *minimum standards* for marriage. I included things like commitment, fidelity, respect, honesty, friendship, self-reliance, and common values.

As I dated girls, I kept my list in mind. I only wanted to get serious with someone who felt comfortable with the standards I considered essential for a successful marriage. At some point—not necessarily on the first date—I would bring up various items to discuss. Shelly, my wife, not only met each of my minimum standards, she exceeded them.

AN EXAMPLE OF A MINOR MINIMUM STANDARD

The following story, although basically true, is told like a parable—not because it had any real significance in our courtship or in our marriage—but because of the valuable lessons it can teach.

One evening after church we were talking about marriage, and I realized I had another item on my list of minimum standards I had not thought about and had not shared with Shelly. It was something trite and immature but nevertheless something on which I did not plan to compromise. That is, I do not eat green beans. I explained that no one forces me to eat green beans, not my mom and not my wife. I asked Shelly how she felt about that.

At first she laughed, never having considered such a thing. Then after she thought about it, she told me that if she went shopping for dinner, came home and prepared, cooked, and served a meal, she would expect her husband to have enough respect and courtesy for her to at least try a little of anything she served. "Yes," she said, "If I served green beans to my husband, I would expect him to have some." I smiled and shook my head, saying, "No, not this husband." We had a little problem. She had a minimum standard I considered unacceptable, and I had a minimum standard she considered unacceptable.

THE DANGER OF CAPITULATION

Perhaps someone would have advised me—for the sake of an otherwise great relationship—to go ahead and eat green beans once a week, even if I did feel like they were being crammed down my throat. But *if* I continued to think I was being forced, feelings of resentment would build week after week. Then, after several years, the problem could escalate beyond a little green bean issue to one of emotional conflict.

Someone might have advised Shelly to simply forego serving green beans at home and order them for herself when out at a restaurant. But *if* she thought she was restricted from serving green beans, she might feel controlled or trapped. If the problem continued unresolved, some degree of stress would be placed on the marriage— not because of green beans per se but because of the accompanying attitudes and feelings.

Just about everyone has at least one green bean dilemma on their list of minimum standards. These little problems in marriage are like slivers in your foot. They may be small, but if ignored they can become infected and cause a great deal of pain. Although most of the things on your list of minimum standards are much more important than green beans, if the little things are not taken care of along with the big things, even the best relationships can deteriorate in time.

Key point: If you have a conflict over a small issue
        that is important to you, resolve it.

WORKING TOWARD A MUTUALLY AGREEABLE SOLUTION

Shelly and I decided to see if we could find a way to respect each other's standard or requirement without capitulating or compromising either one's integrity. Even though it was a little problem, it took us an hour and a half to resolve it. But it was worth it. First of all, neither of us ridiculed or attempted to pressure the other to change his position. I especially appreciated that because I knew I was not coming from the most rational and mature place. Shelly was the one who finally proposed the solution that, to this day, works. In a kind way and with a smile on her face, she said, "John, if you will tell me, *ahead of time*, what food you are too immature to eat, I will only serve that food to the children and me. Would that be all right?" That sounded great to me.

SOME ADVICE

I encourage all single adults, regardless of age or circumstance, to *write* their minimum standards for marriage. Then, when the time comes to make one of the most important decisions in life, they will not be left to rely on their emotions alone. They will have an objective criteria to assist them in deciding whether or not marrying a particular person is a wise decision. A wise prophet once said, "The decision to marry is best made with 90% head and 10% heart."

For those who are already married, it is not too late. You can still list your minimum standards and discuss them with your spouse. Many marital problems can be resolved simply by clarifying your standards and working toward a way to respect each others basic requirements.

Setting Minimum Standards for Relatives

Vance and Sobrina loved Vance's parents and enjoyed their visits—which occurred several times a year. The grandparents were an important part of their family. They helped with the down payment on the house and spent a lot of time caring for and playing with the children. The only problem was that Vance and Sobrina did not drink or serve alcohol in their home, and Grandpa was an alcoholic who brought his jug of wine whenever he visited. The situation was discussed, debated, and ignored for years. Vance and Sabrina never took a firm stand.

> *Key point*: Without clear and firm minimum standards, it is difficult to take a stand in a relationship. You thereby become susceptible to capitulation or manipulation.

Asking Grandpa to not drink seemed unthinkable, yet having him continue to drink in front of the children was unacceptable. Vance and Sobrina felt they were in a bind. They asked me to help them find an acceptable way to tell Grandpa not to bring alcohol into their home. I pointed out that they were asking me to help them accomplish two things, one of which they could control and the other they could not. Finding a kind, honest, and constructive way to communicate their wishes to Grandpa was definitely achievable. Whether or not he responded to their request in a reasonable or unreasonable manner was out of their control.

YOU HAVE THE RIGHT TO SET YOUR OWN STANDARDS FOR A RELATIONSHIP

I explained to Vance and Sobrina that they have the right to determine the standards for acceptable behavior in their home for children, parents, or guests. It was their choice. The decision not to have alcohol in their home was easy for them, but they were still worried about how their parents would react.

Vance was afraid Grandpa would feel rejected, unappreciated, and possibly never visit them again. I understood Vance's concern. Nevertheless, I reassured him that when Grandpa is given the choice between visiting his family without bringing his jug or not visiting his family, I expected he would find a way to accept his son's standard. Even if Grandpa was upset at first, he would probably get over it. I reminded him that blood is thicker than alcohol.

TAKING A STAND

With fear and trembling (Thanksgiving was a month away and grandparents were planning to visit) Vance and Sobrina wrote a letter with three parts. *First*, they sincerely expressed their love and appreciation to their parents. *Second*, they explained their family policy of no alcohol in their home and kindly stated that Grandpa would no longer be able to drink in their home—of course, what he did outside of their home was up to him. *Third*, they shared their hopes for a continued close and loving relationship.

Fortunately, I had prepared them for the worst. A week after sending the letter, Vance and Sobrina received a note saying, "After all we have done for you, you treat us like this. We know when we are not wanted. We will never step foot in your home again." I reviewed with them their right to set the standards in their home and the grandparents' right to accept or reject those standards. No one was rejecting anybody. The grandparents were struggling—albeit not very gracefully—with how to deal with their adult children's rules in much the same way a child might struggle with parents' rules. I reminded Vance and Sobrina that misinterpretation, tantrums, and rebellion are not limited to two-year-olds and teenagers.

The End Result—A Better Relationship

When the grandparents did not visit over Thanksgiving, it was all Vance and Sobrina could do to resist giving in. It just broke their heart thinking of losing the closeness their family had previously enjoyed. I reassured them that I have never seen grandparents permanently disown their children or cease to associate with them, when the children take a firm yet reasonable stand. I have assisted over one hundred adult children to respectfully announce to parents that certain behaviors were unacceptable (behaviors such as giving unsolicited advice, making critical comments, dropping in unannounced, and criticizing the adult children's child-raising practices). Although it is possible for parents to be so proud or disturbed that they would reject their own flesh and blood over some issue, it is extremely unlikely.

About two weeks before Christmas a wonderful letter arrived. Grandpa and Grandma announced they would be coming for Christmas without their jug of wine. At the end of the visit, Grandpa told Bill they had a great time—in fact, a better time than usual. The family had progressed through a difficult and awkward stage. Now the relationship was more mature and more loving than before.

SETTING MINIMUM STANDARDS IN THE WORKPLACE

Kyle was the vice-president of a large national corporation. Even though he was working sixty to eighty hours a week, there was always more to do. Although his boss (the president) was pleased, he kept pushing Kyle for greater and greater performance. Kyle found himself suffering with frequent headaches and a deteriorating home life.

I asked Kyle whether or not he felt he was doing a good job. Even though his boss was pleased and profits were up significantly from the previous year, he did not feel that he was doing a good job. In fact, he even worried about being fired. He also worried about losing his family whom he loved deeply. He knew he could not continue to work at his current pace but feared the wrath of his boss.

I suggested he write his minimum standards for an acceptable performance. At first he was concerned that I wanted him to be satisfied with a mediocre performance. I emphasized the importance of having lofty goals and sincerely striving to obtain them. I also explained that measuring his performance against an ideal standard was self-defeating. Once he understood, he made a thorough and detailed list of what he was willing and able to do for his company. One of the items was work fifty hours a week—with exceptions only on rare occasions.

Although he sincerely believed he might be fired after presenting his standards, for the sake of his family and his health he set up an appointment with his boss. First, he assured the president he was fully committed to the mission and goals of the company. Then he presented his boss with the list of his standards, asking if performance at such a level would be acceptable. He decided not to use the word "minimum" because he thought it might be misunderstood to mean mediocre.

As generally happens, the boss reviewed the list of standards, finding them *more* than satisfactory. Another interesting thing happened. By carefully analyzing the needs of the company and his own talents, Bill prioritized and organized his efforts in a way that he could be more productive in less time. Not only did Kyle end up with more time for himself and his family, he made a more significant contribution to his company .

Reminder: *If this central principle does not apply to your particular concern, go to another central principle OR go directly to the section on the problem you wish to solve: Communication Difficulties, Depression, Unsatisfactory Intimacy, or Anxiety Attacks.*

PRINCIPLE 8

CARE FOR YOUR PHYSICAL HEALTH

The health of your mind, body, and emotions depends on proper and consistent nutrition, exercise, and sleep. Strive to eat moderately, exercise regularly, and get sufficient sleep.

Rule of thumb: Eat three well-balanced, low-fat meals a day, exercise 20-30 minutes, three to four times a week; and sleep seven to nine hours a night.

GENERAL INFORMATION

It is common knowledge your body needs proper exercise, rest, and good nutrition to function effectively; otherwise, you feel weak and fatigued. Your brain—like a muscle—has physical needs the same as your body. If you fail to take good care of your body, your mind will not be at its best.

If your body or mind is in a weakened state, you naturally tend to think about or view life in an unclear, negative, or exaggerated manner. Insufficient food, exercise, or rest, is a common cause or contributing factor when you are feeling upset, depressed, anxious, or angry.

STEPS TO APPLYING THE PRINCIPLE

1. Examine your eating habits. Are you getting three well-balanced meals a day? Are you eating moderately, especially products containing large quantities of fat, sugar, or salt? Are you habitually taking anything into your body which artificially affects your emotions such as caffeine, alcohol, or tobacco?

2. Examine your sleeping habits. Are you getting the sleep your body requires at this particular time of your life? (Different amounts of sleep are required, depending on age, circumstance, and stress level.) Do you have a fairly regular routine for bedtime and for getting up?

3. Try an experiment. Decide on some manageable improvements you would like to make in your eating and sleeping habits. Practice your improvements for 30 days, then see how much better you feel.

4. Examine your exercise habits. Are you getting a minimum of 20 minutes of good cardiovascular exercise such as walking, running, swimming, or cycling 3 to 4 times a week ?

   If you are not exercising regularly, remind yourself that regular, moderate exercise is good for you, regardless of how you feel.*

   Consider various ways you could exercise. If you need ideas ask a family member, friend, or librarian; or check local college, YMCA, church, and community groups for exercise classes.

---

* Consult your physician first if you have not been exercising regularly in the last year or if you have health concerns.

Decide on an exercise plan best for you. Set up a regular schedule (6:00-6:30 a.m., Monday, Wednesday, and Friday for example). If you have difficulty beginning or continuing on your own, join with a friend or a group.

5. While you are exercising, notice how much easier it is to avoid feeling upset.

6. Continue your exercise program, even if you are not yet feeling better. The added strength you are gaining will help you in taking whatever additional actions are advisable.

PERSONAL APPLICATION

At first glance it was not difficult to see why Martha was depressed. She was going through a painful divorce, her son was getting into fights at school and refusing to obey at home, and there was hardly enough money to make ends meet. She sought help for herself. Although a counselor helped her more effectively deal with the divorce and her son, she still felt depressed.

When she came to me seeking additional help, I asked her, among other things, to tell me about her nutritional, exercise, and sleep habits. She told me there was so much to do she could only get about five hours of sleep a night. To wake up in the morning and stay awake at work, she drank about six caffeine beverages a day. She was too busy to eat more than one or two meals a day although she usually found a way to grab a candy bar or donut now and then. As far as exercise, that was the last thing she felt like doing.

Although I suspected a variety of causes and solutions for her depression, I told her I would only accept her as a client if she committed to do the following: eat three meals a day, get seven to eight hours of sleep a night, and dramatically decrease her caffeine consumption, if not eliminate it entirely.

> *Reason*: Until she took better care of her body, she was not likely to escape feeling depressed, no matter how many improvements she made in other areas of her life.

Although Martha was not happy about what I required of her, she made the commitment. She then proceeded to tell me she thought she needed some antidepression medication. I explained that in some cases such medication is appropriate, but even then only as a temporary aid until the mind and body are functioning better and until the person being treated has learned the skills to live more effectively. I told her we could consider the possibility that she might need medication, but before I would recommend it, I wanted her to do what she could herself to restore her physical health.

She agreed. She began taking daily walks, sometimes early in the morning or during her lunch hour at work. At first, the exercise was a chore—one more thing for her to do—but soon she began to find it somewhat enjoyable.

Although it took more than proper nutrition, exercise, and sleep for Martha to climb out of her pit of depression, doing those things gave her the physical strength necessary to make the climb and in her case, she succeeded without the use of medication

> **Reminder**: *If this central principle does not apply to your particular concern, go to another central principle OR, go directly to the section on the problem you wish to solve: Communication Difficulties, Depression, Unsatisfactory Intimacy, or Anxiety Attacks.*

COMMUNICATION
DIFFICULTIES

OVERVIEW

In some ways communication is so simple that even children learn without being formally taught. On the other hand I still find that learning to communicate successfully requires regular attention and practice.

Some people were fortunate enough to be raised in families where good communication skills were taught and practiced. To such individuals communication may not seem too difficult because they were taught correct principles and continue practicing them daily. Many others, however, were either not taught, or for some reason did not learn to communicate effectively. Regardless of your upbringing, you could not have made it this far in life without learning to communicate effectively in at least one area or another. Unfortunately, however, effective communication is often least evident where it matters most.

Many good, sensitive, and intelligent people communicate well in professional or social situations, but not in intimate personal relationships. Such individuals may be puzzled why they can communicate so well with people they do not care so much about, but not with those they love. One woman could not comprehend how her husband could be a great business leader and yet be unable to communicate with her or with their children. This woman, usually patient and understanding with others, became easily hurt or angry with her husband, making communication even more difficult.

Many people do not realize there are two versions of any given language: one used in non-intimate settings, such as work and social, and the other used in intimate, personal settings such as family. A highly skilled engineer, for example, may be fluent in non-intimate, technical communication, yet inexperienced and unskilled in intimate family communication. Or, a person highly skilled in intimate communication, may struggle with anything that seems technical.

Usually, those with communication difficulties have sincerely tried, at least on occasion, to share their feelings in a sensitive and understanding manner. However, when they failed and experienced more pain, rejection, and misunderstanding, they understandably began avoiding intimate communication. They simply put up a wall or turned themselves off emotionally. As a result, barriers developed that interfered with communication where it matters most.

If you have not yet learned to communicate in intimate relationships, there is hope. Fortunately, the principles of good communication are the same whether in a business, social, or personal situation. You can learn to identify and apply those communication principles successfully used in other areas of your life to an intimate relationship. Then, the communication skills developed and utilized elsewhere will begin to surface and grow where they effect your life most.

Suggestion: If your companion is willing, try reading this chapter out loud together. Each time you finish reading a portion, decide what specific actions you would like to take to improve the way you communicate.

COMMUNICATION

One of the most important aspects of human relationships is the ability to communicate ideas and feelings in a clear and effective manner. Learning to communicate effectively is an essential ingredient in a healthy relationship whether with family, friends, or business associates. Unfortunately, sometimes people attempt or even force communication in circumstances unlikely to be successful. How well can you carry on a good discussion, for example, if the other person is being unkind, not completely open, or is dishonest? It is highly unlikely communication will be successful under such circumstances, and it may even be harmful. In order to promote good communication three rules are recommended:

> 1. *Be Kind.*
> 2. *Be Honest.*
> 3. *Have Constructive Intent.*

ALL THREE RULES ARE ESSENTIAL

All three rules, not just one or two, are essential for good communication. To be kind without also being straightforward and honest would be of little value; and to be honest without being kind could be brutal. Likewise, if your intentions are not constructive but appear to be kind and honest, good communication will not be promoted. These three rules are simple and obvious but can be difficult to adhere to under stressful circumstances.

By following these rules a bridge of trust is built between you and your companion. A safe, fertile, and trusting environment is established where problems can be resolved and closeness fostered. Arguments become a thing of the past as you learn to disagree without being disagreeable. Misunderstandings do not degenerate into arguments because conversations are politely postponed when one or more of the Three Rules are continually violated.

As you and your companion agree to and apply the Three Rules, you are taking giant steps toward building a strong, trusting relationship. Sometimes, however, one of you may agree in principle, but find it difficult to follow through in practice.

> *Caution:* If only one person is applying the Three Rules, he may be falsely accused of refusing to communicate or of attempting to control the relationship.

DISAGREEMENT OVER THE THREE RULES

When there is disagreement over the Three Rules, whether in principle or practice, it is important to realize you have certain rights, independent of what anyone else thinks. You have the right to determine the conditions under which you are willing to carry on a conversation. You can decide, for example, to only participate in conversations where the Three Rules are kept. You do not, however, have the right to force another person to adhere to the same rules. If someone wishes to violate the Three Rules, that is his right, but he does not have the right to force you to participate. When the Three Rules are violated you have the right to kindly postpone the conversation, even leave the room if necessary, regardless of what the other person thinks.

Until two people can agree and generally abide by the same set of rules for communication, there is little chance they will communicate effectively. Some people have become so accustomed to violating one or more of the Three Rules, that adhering to them can feel restrictive at first. In fact, it is not uncommon for a couple to be concerned that if they follow the Three Rules they may hardly ever talk.

Key point: It is much better, at first, to talk successfully less often, than to continue talking ineffectively more often.

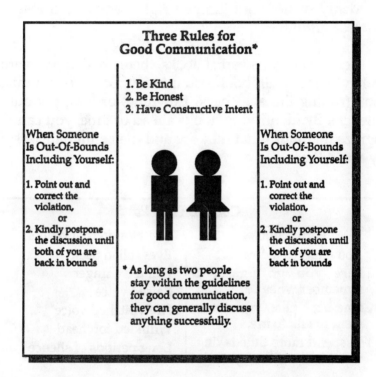

Three Rules for Good Communication*

1. Be Kind
2. Be Honest
3. Have Constructive Intent

When Someone Is Out-Of-Bounds Including Yourself:

1. Point out and correct the violation,
   or
2. Kindly postpone the discussion until both of you are back in bounds

When Someone Is Out-Of-Bounds Including Yourself:

1. Point out and correct the violation,
   or
2. Kindly postpone the discussion until both of you are back in bounds

* As long as two people stay within the guidelines for good communication, they can generally discuss anything successfully.

INVITATIONS TO VIOLATE THE THREE RULES

Despite the best intentions of sensitive and responsible people, violating one or more of the Three Rules is easy. Certain things your companion says or does—often innocently—can hook and pull you out-of- bounds before you know it. Some of these hooks are so alluring they almost seem irresistible.

Example: When Dale yelled at Janice for not picking up the clothes he left on the floor, she politely told him she would discuss the matter if he would talk nicely—within the Three Rules. When he continued to yell and blame, she started to leave the room. Then came the hook: "There you go again, running away from responsibility. You know you are wrong, so you refuse to discuss it." Janice suddenly turned and jumped right back into a lose-lose argument.

Besides obvious verbal hooks, there are also non-verbal behaviors that can hook you into ineffective communication (rolling the eyes back, frowning, or long periods of silence). By identifying hooks ahead of time, you can recognize them for what they are and then eliminate or safely avoid them.

Common Hooks	
Verbal hooks	**Non-verbal hooks**
If you really loved me . . .	Eyes rolled back
There you go again. I remember when . . .	Pointed a finger
	Raised voice
Come back here, you never want to talk to me.	High pitched voice
	Wrinkled forehead
You spend more time taking care of others than you do us.	Long periods of silence
You never . . .	
You always . . .	
You are trying to control me.	
Well, if you are going to be *that* way about it . . .	
If you really cared about the way I feel . . .	
If you were a good wife, mother, etc . . .	
You care more about . . . than you care about me.	
You do not know what you are talking about.	

If you decide to adhere to the Three Rules and find yourself having difficulty, here is a suggestion. Make a list of things your companion says or does that tend to hook you into conversations you know are not constructive. See the list of *Common Hooks* on the previous page.

Be patient! If you have had a lot of practice getting hooked, it will take some time to learn to resist the temptation. One client found it helpful to create a visual image of a sugar-coated hook dangling from the end of his wife's tongue. Just the thought made him laugh. (Even though he enjoyed the picture, I suggested he restrain himself from laughing when his wife was upset.)

With practice anyone can learn to communicate within the Three Rules for Good Communication, and knowing these rules will help in identifying and removing the barriers to effective communication.

Barriers to Overcoming Communication Difficulties

Nine common barriers interfere with overcoming communication difficulties. By identifying and removing barriers, you will be in a better position to practice and develop the kind of communication skills you desire.

Barrier 1: Unclear rules for communication

Barrier 2: Difficulty distinguishing thoughts and feelings from facts

Barrier 3: Difficulty distinguishing between what you can and cannot control

Barrier 4: Difficulty focusing attention on your companion

Barrier 5: Trying to get your companion to communicate better

Barrier 6: Making excuses for your companion

Barrier 7: Blaming yourself for his excessive criticism

Barrier 8: Basing your security or happiness on your companion

Barrier 9: Not knowing how to proceed with a companion who will not cooperate

Unclear Rules for Communication

COMMON INDICATORS

Thoughts: "I expect better communication, but regardless of what I say or do, he continues to communicate in ways I consider inappropriate or unacceptable."

"I cannot stand it when he belittles me, but if I walk away he'll get mad at me."

Feelings: Frustrated, confused, inadequate, resentful.

Actions: Participating in conversations—actively or passively—that are non-productive or disrespectful. Examples: (1) Continuing to talk, even though he is not listening. (2) Passively listening while he speaks unkindly. (3) Speaking unkindly because he. . . .

GENERAL INFORMATION

Everyone has his own personal rules or standards for effective communication, whether conscious of them or not. If you are not aware of or comfortable with your standards, you cannot take a stand or have your stand respected. Consequently effective communication becomes difficult or impossible. Often, two people attempt to communicate without clearly defined and mutually agreed upon rules. Therefore they inadvertently risk stepping on each other's toes or, at the least, communicating ineffectively.

> *Example:* The first time Curtis and Catherine came to my office, Catherine explained at length and in great detail about the communication problems they were having. Curtis hardly said a word. Finally, when I asked for his opinion, he began to explain, "If I say something she does not like, she mouths off . . ." She quickly interjected, "I may mouth off at times, but his mouth is always off."

As you and your companion clarify and agree on the basic rules for effective communication (the Three Rules For Good Communication), a common barrier to effective communication is removed.

STEPS TO REMOVING THE BARRIER

1. Consider what will be different when you and your companion are communicating better. Think of times in the past when communication was successful. What was different during those times?

   Example: As Lee struggled to recall times when he and Joyce were *not* arguing or avoiding each other, he discovered some interesting things. First, there actually were times when they got along better. Second, he came up with some things he could do differently to communicate better. Third, he began to feel more hopeful.

2. Consider what guidelines or standards you believe to be absolutely essential for effective communication. You might find it helpful to write down your ideas. A good place to begin is with the Three Rules for Good Communication—Be kind, Be Honest, and Have Con-

structive Intent. Make sure you include any additional rules you consider essential for good communication (such as discussing sensitive topics *only* when hunger, fatigue, and time are not issues).

Note: If you are concerned that certain conversations tend to last longer than you wish, try setting a time limit (thirty minutes or so).

3. After you have completed your list, go back and elaborate on each item you consider essential for good communication. Be specific and include examples. For instance, what do you mean by kind? How will you know when he is treating you kindly?.

Example: Walter was accustomed to telling Carol what he thought she "should" or "shouldn't" do. In his mind, there was nothing disrespectful or unkind about his language. Carol, however, interpreted words like "should," "must," "cannot," and "have to," as coercive. It was not a matter of who was right. The important fact is that effective communication can only occur when *both* agree they are being treated kindly.

Solution: Either Walter uses different words ("I prefer" rather than, "You should") or Carol can remind herself his use of the word "Should" is not intended to be demanding or coercive.

4. After identifying and clarifying your rules for good communication, evaluate yourself according to your own standards. Notice where you are doing well and where you would like to improve.

5. Before you share your list with your companion, invite him to read this chapter and privately make up his own rules for good communication. Meanwhile, work on living up to your own standards.

6. After he has completed his list, and if he is willing, compare notes. If he does not want to read this chapter or make a list, but you believe he has given some thought to his guidelines, proceed anyway.

    Caution: If he is not clear on his guidelines and you are clear on yours, he may feel he is being controlled or manipulated.

    Remember: As long as you are not trying to control him, any feelings he may have to the contrary do not change the facts.

7. In discussing your rules, emphasize the mutually agreed upon points.

    Important: Do not assume you know what the other means. Remember the meaning of "ASSUME" (making an ASS out of U and ME). Do not try to be a mind reader no matter how good you seem to be at it. *Instead,* ask questions. A good question to ask is "What do you mean by that?" After you both understand what each other's rules are, you will probably find them quite similar.

    Note: Differences are more likely to reflect different points of view toward the same thing rather than fundamental differences. One person may provide a long, highly detailed list while the other provides a short, concise list covering the most important points. If you discover major differences that cannot be resolved in a mutually satisfactory manner, consider seeking professional help. (See Appendix, "How To Select A Therapist.")

8. Whenever one of you appears to be violating a mutually agreed upon rule, signal time-out— place hands together to form a "T"—then kindly point out the violation. If both of you can agree and get back in bounds, the discussion can continue successfully; otherwise, kindly postpone the discussion to a later time. Agree in advance to use the "time-out" signal only when you sincerely care about your companion and are committed to improving the relationship.

Result: Calling time-out will be defined as an act of love rather than rejection or avoidance. Before you know it, you will both fit like a "T."

Example:

Ron: "Your voice seems to be getting a little loud. I think we're getting outside of the 'Three Rules.'"

Kathy: "You are right, I'm sorry."

Conversation continues.

Example:

Georgia: "I get the feeling you are trying to make me agree with you."

Mike: "You know I am right when it comes to disciplining the children."

Georgia (Time Out signal): "Mike, I love you and look forward to discussing this matter

when we both can be more open-minded."
Georgia then politely left the room, even
though Mike wanted to continue the "discussion."

Result: Whether or not your companion agrees
with your methods, you will eliminate arguments.

Important: Do not forget to follow up on any
postponed discussions at a later time.

With patience and practice, you will find it easier and easier to communicate by the rules you
have set.

Difficulty Distinguishing Thoughts and Feelings from Facts

COMMON INDICATORS

Thoughts: "This is the way it is." "She does not know what she is talking about."

Feelings: Unusually strong feelings attached to opinions.

Actions: Difficulty listening to and accepting others' viewpoints. Jumping to conclusions. Incorrectly assuming you know what someone else is thinking or feeling.

GENERAL INFORMATION

In order to communicate effectively, it is necessary to clearly label an opinion an opinion, a feeling a feeling, and a fact a fact. Then facts are easily agreed upon, which sets the stage for respecting, understanding, and discussing each others thoughts and feelings.

If, however, you strongly believe that your thoughts or feelings accurately represent the facts when in fact they do not, it becomes difficult, if not impossible, to reason with yourself or with others. When you observe another person's words and actions and assume you know more than you actually know (their private thoughts, feelings, or motives), misunderstandings will naturally result.

Consider, for instance, two people discussing the merits of a particular fruit, where one is basing his opinions on apples and the other is basing her opinions on oranges. If each thinks they are talking about the same fruit, try as they might, they will not be able to understand each other's opinions and feelings. He may talk about enjoying the crunchiness of the fruit, while she might insist it was not crunchy at all, but rather, soft and juicy. He may insist peeling the fruit was optional, while she might think he was crazy to think such a thing. They could argue about the rightness or wrongness of each other's opinion indefinitely and still not understand or agree.

STEPS TO REMOVING THE BARRIER

1. Compare situations where communication seems successful versus unsuccessful. Notice situations where communication goes well and opinions, feelings, and facts are clearly differentiated and labelled.

Examples:

Opinion stated as fact: "It takes too long to watch a baseball game"

Better: "It usually takes about three hours for a nine-inning baseball game to be played [Fact]. That's longer than I am comfortable with [Opinion]."

Opinion stated as fact: "You are a reckless driver."

Better: "Although you have never been in an accident, you do tend to exceed the speed limit [Facts], and I feel uncomfortable when you do so [Feeling/Opinion]."

Opinion stated as fact: "You are a good cook."

Better: "I like the way you cook [Opinion]."

2. In your conversations, practice clearly labelling an opinion as an opinion, a feeling as a feeling, and a fact as a fact.

   Key point: Use words that indicate a fact only when describing objective facts. Watch for the words listed below which describe thoughts and feelings, and compare them to the words that suggest fact.

Thinking and Feeling Words	Fact Words
I think . . .	It is . . .
I feel . . .	You are . .
I like . . .	I know . . .
I believe . . .	You are feeling . . .
I prefer . . .	You are thinking . . .
It seems to me . . .	
It appears to me . . .	
It is apt . . .	
It might . . .	
My point of view . . .	
My feeling is . . .	
My opinion is . . .	

For additional information, please see Central Principle 3: "Feelings versus Facts," page 40.

3. Practice with your companion distinguishing thoughts and feelings from facts

   • Agree to practice on a topic you have both had difficulty discussing.

Caution: Do not select an extremely controversial situation.

- Agree on the objective facts of the situation. You may wish to write down the facts you come up with.

Key point: Agreeing on the facts is a basic and critical element of effective communication and initially may take the most effort. Discussing thoughts and feelings before you agree on the facts is apt to be counterproductive.

- Discuss your thoughts and feelings about those facts, using the Three Rules for Good Communication (Be Kind, Be Honest, and Have Constructive Intent).

Result: As you improve in distinguishing thoughts and feelings from facts, you will discover more opportunities for agreement as well as ways to disagree without being disagreeable.

Difficulty Distinguishing Between What You Can and Cannot Control

COMMON INDICATORS

Thoughts: "If I improve myself—lose some weight or something—*then* he will be more interested in talking to me."

"I will not criticize her for one week, *then* she will be more affectionate."

"After all I have done, why isn't he more sensitive and open?"

Feelings: Helpless, easily upset, overly confident that all is well

Actions: Trying too hard to make communication go just right. Taking on too much or too little responsibility for communication.

GENERAL INFORMATION

In any relationship, there is a line that divides what you can control from what you cannot control. When that line is clear and each person takes responsibility for what he can control, effective communication is encouraged. When that line is unclear, a person often mistakenly focuses on and attempts to control things he cannot control. Besides obvious and disrespectful methods of manipulation, there is another type of control that is often unconscious and unintentional but just as damaging. This type of control is not a visible behavior; it occurs in the mind. It most often occurs when you believe you are responsible for causing or controlling what someone else thinks, feels, or does.

Result: Mental and emotional energy needlessly go down the drain and a power struggle often results over who controls what.

Example: When Sara is angry, she believes Todd made her feel that way. Her only options then are to fight or flee. She mistakenly focuses on Todd's behavior, which she cannot control, thinking *he* must change in order for her to feel better. A solution would be to focus on what you can do to contribute to better communication or, at the very least, not to make poor communication worse.

Thinking about trying to control someone you cannot control is like banging heads. You hurt not only yourself, but your companion as well. Whether your companion is conscious of your intentions or not, he will likely feel you are trying to control him even when your actions are above reproach.

Example: Laverne worked very hard all week long not to complain about anything to Ray.

Mistake: She believed controlling her behavior—a commendable thing to do—would somehow cause Ray to better control his behavior.

Example: James was determined to have peace in his home no matter what. He would not talk about anything he thought Melinda might get upset about.

Mistake: He was trying to promote peace—a worthwhile objective—by preventing Melinda from becoming upset.

Result: They talked very little or superficially; problems mounted rather than being resolved and Melinda felt James did not care about her feelings.

Fact: James cared so much about Melinda's feelings that he was carrying responsibility for controlling them.

Key point: It is the underlying motive, purpose, or intent of a your actions as well as the actions themselves that are so often controlling.

People who try to overcome behaving in controlling ways often fail because they only attempt to restrain their actions rather than examine and correct their underlying intentions. Those who rarely behave in controlling ways but who nevertheless have controlling thoughts tend to ignore or resist any suggestions that they are being controlling. Hence, they have difficulty improving how they communicate.

STEPS TO REMOVING THE BARRIER

1. When you are thinking about a situation with your companion where one or both of you are upset, focus your attention on what you can control rather than on what you cannot control.

> Ask yourself:
>
> *"What aspects of this situation can I control* and what aspects can't I control?"

Briefly describe the facts of the situation on paper as a video camera would record them (no opinions, feelings, or interpretations). Then draw a line down the center of the paper. On one side of the line write aspects of the situation you can control, and on the other side aspects you cannot control.

Example: Ken arrived home one hour later than he promised. Irene was upset. With a harsh voice, she said, "I've been waiting for over an hour. You are so selfish and inconsiderate that I can't believe I put up with you." Ken was confused and upset. With all the self-control he could muster, he politely told Irene he would be willing to discuss the matter after dinner when, hopefully, they could both talk within the Three Rules for Good Communication. He then left the room. To help him straighten out his thinking, he made a list of what he could and could not control in the situation.

Ken's List	
Can Control	**Cannot Control**
The time I say I'll be home	Traffic conditions
When I leave for home	Irene's mistaken belief I am always late and that I do not care about her feelings
Whether or not I call if I am going to be late	
Whether or not I apologize	Her blood pressure
How I react to Irene's behavior	Her voice tone
	Her belief that I am responsible for how she is feeling.

Result: By drawing a clear and detailed line between what Ken could and could not control, he was able to relieve himself of accepting responsibility for the things he could not control while more fully accepting responsibility for the things he could control. He was excited to discover that he did not have to argue, defend, or condemn himself when Irene was upset. Instead, he decided to concentrate on being prompt and kindly postponing unhealthy conversations even though Irene misunderstood and felt upset at first.

2. Consider some of the things bothering you about the way you and your companion communicate. On another piece of paper with a line down the center, put the things you can control on one side of the line and the things you cannot control on the other side.

3. Select one thing on your list that bothers you that you can control. Make and implement a plan for doing something about it.

4. When you find yourself dwelling on some aspect of communication you cannot control, watch what happens; do not try to change your thinking at first. Just notice the consequences. Note especially how you tend to feel and act.

5. Examine your thoughts, especially when you or your companion are feeling uncomfortable or agitated. Practice distinguishing your controlling thoughts from your respectful thoughts. Be careful! Controlling thoughts—like counterfeit money—often look and feel like the real thing, but they are not.

   Controlling: "If I do what he wants, *then* he will do what I want."

   Respectful: "If I do what he wants, there is an increased likelihood or probability, he will choose to do what I want him to."

   Controlling: "If I act a certain way, *then* he will feel a certain way."

   Respectful: "If I act a certain way, he is more likely to feel ..."

   Controlling: "I upset him."

   Respectful: "I am responsible for my actions, and he is responsible for his reactions."

Result: By increasing your awareness of whether you are focusing on what you can or cannot control and the results that follow, your mind will naturally tend to focus more on things you can control.

Warning: Just because your companion thinks or feels you are trying to control him does not necessarily mean you are doing so.

Key point: Feelings do not change facts. Nevertheless, if your companion is feeling controlled, carefully examine your thoughts and underlying motives to see if anything is amiss.

6. When you are dwelling on things you cannot control ask yourself, "Do I really want to be thinking about this?" If not, practice thinking about or doing something you do have control over.

Result: You will create an environment where, in time, better communication is much more likely.

Difficulty Focusing Attention on Your Companion

COMMON INDICATORS

Thoughts: "I'd rather be doing something else, but I better at least look like I am paying attention. I can carry on a conversation while thinking about something else."

Feelings: Torn between two or more conflicting interests; stress.

Actions: Talking or listening to someone while thinking about or doing something else. Not looking at someone while they are talking.

GENERAL INFORMATION

Focusing your attention on the person with whom you are talking includes frequent eye contact, relevant comments, and avoiding distractions such as T.V., newspapers, and magazines. However, these actions alone—though important—are not enough to produce effective communication. It is also necessary to focus your thoughts and mental activity on the person. This is not always easy. Given all the pressures, responsibilities, interruptions, and distractions of life, it takes a great deal of effort and practice to give the quality of attention necessary to communicate effectively.

Example: Richard's wife and children liked to talk with him during breakfast. Although he loved his family deeply, he liked to read the newspaper during breakfast. His strategy was to do both at the same time. He could hear and answer their questions, while he also read the paper.

Problem: His family wondered how important they were to him, and he felt torn.

Solution: Do one or the other. Richard could put the paper down for a few minutes and give his family his undivided attention. Or he could ask them to allow him a few minutes to read the paper without interruption.

The amount of attention you give someone during a conversation can range from zero to one hundred percent. When you give one hundred percent of your attention, you will think, feel, and communicate better. In addition, the other person will be apt to feel and appreciate your full attention.

STEPS TO REMOVING THE BARRIER

1. Monitor on a scale of zero to one hundred the percent of attention you are giving various people and situations in your life.

> Ask yourself,
>
> *"How much attention am I giving to the current situation?"*

For instance, Richard might have answered seventy percent attention to the newspaper and thirty percent to the family. Consider how much attention you give in other situations (talking with a business associate, watching T.V., playing tennis, or listening to a sermon). Observe how the amount of attention you give varies depending on how much interest, energy, and self-discipline you have at the moment. Your increased awareness will allow you to give more attention to the current situation.

2. Give your companion permission to ask how much attention you are giving her at the moment.

Example: While riding in the car, LaVonne was telling Robert about her day. LaVonne wondered how much attention he was paying to what she was saying. Rather than assuming he was or was not listening, she said, "Robert, how much attention are you giving to what I am saying?"

Result: If Robert was not paying full attention, he might just begin to do so now that LaVonne has mentioned it. Or if he feels he really cannot fully listen at the moment, he could politely tell her he has so much on his mind he would rather talk later.

Important: Make sure to follow-up with the conversation at a later time.

3. Your choice: If your companion has the habit of not giving his full attention, you can interpret his behavior as something he is doing "to me." This results in hurt feelings or anger, leading to fleeing or fighting. Or you can interpret his behavior as a difficulty he has with personal communication, even if he seems to have little or no trouble paying attention in other situations.

Key Point: Regardless of how you interpret his behavior, you have the right, if you wish, to participate only in conversations where both of you are giving your full attention.

4. When talking with your companion—especially when there is some discomfort or tension.

> Ask yourself,
>
> *"How much attention am I giving to my companion versus the topic of discussion?"*

Example: One day when I was in graduate school, I was sharing some supposedly profound things I learned with my wife, Shelly. She listened intently for quite awhile. Then she told me she felt like I was giving a lecture—that I was more interested in the topic than with her. Her comment surprised me and I assured her she was certainly more important to me than whatever I was talking about. She was not convinced, however.

I then took another look. I asked myself whether I was paying more attention to my topic or to her. I was humbled by my discovery. Despite my initial belief to the contrary, I was, in fact, more involved and excited about my ideas than I was about my wife at that moment.

5. Remind yourself that the person you are talking with at any given time is more important than whatever you are talking about. Of course, the topic or information is important, but your companion's thoughts, feelings, and your relationship is of greater importance.

Trying to Get Your Companion to Communicate Better

COMMON INDICATORS

Thoughts: "How can I get through to him . . . to get him to listen to me, talk with me, accept me, and understand me?" "Why won't he . . . ?"

Feelings: Discouraged, frustrated, helpless, upset.

Actions: Coming on too strong. Walking on eggs so as not to upset him. Violating your own rules for good communication.

GENERAL INFORMATION

Wanting better communication can inadvertently develop into an attitude of trying too hard to get it. The intent to have better communication can inadvertently lead to manipulation. If, for instance, your companion is unable or unwilling to communicate better at the present time, any intent on your part *to make* him improve is apt to be disrespectful and will only make matters worse. Besides, if you push too long or too hard *you* may end up looking like the one who cannot communicate effectively.

Example: Art frequently complained that Vicki was trying to control him. In order to help Art realize she was not trying to control him, Vicki carefully examined every word before she spoke, making sure he could not possibly misinterpret her intentions. She walked on eggs because she tried so hard not to upset him. Despite her best efforts he would still become upset and accuse her of trying to control him. Her resulting frustration led her to try so hard to get him to admit she was not trying to control him that she inadvertently ended up doing the very thing she sincerely wanted to avoid—she tried to control Art.

Example: David had the habit of regularly putting his wife down. The harder Wanda tried to get him to treat her more respectfully, the more critical he became. David, too, wanted to be kinder, but often his habit was more powerful than his desire to be gentle. Besides, he viewed some of Wanda's efforts to get him to change as controlling and he was not going to let anyone run his life. I suggested an approach to them that they both accepted that broke the bind they were in. Wanda agreed to stop trying so hard to get him to treat her better. David agreed to give her $1 each time he criticized her without first giving her a genuine compliment. The following week Wanda smiled and said to David, "Why did you have to change your habit so fast? I thought I would get rich."

Even in situations where your companion is not initially as responsive as David is in the previous example, it is still essential to respect his *right* to communicate ineffectively—even though that certainly is not your preference. It is also essential to respect your right to consider your options and do what you think is best when communication is not going well. For example, you have the right to periodically ask him if he is ready to work toward better communication. Even when he is not yet ready, you can continue hoping he will someday change his mind. In the meantime, remember: You do not have to participate in conversations that violate your rules for effective communication. Rather than trying too hard *to get* your companion to communicate better there is a lot you can do *to give* him greater opportunities to do so.

> *Key Point:* The attitude or intent underlying your actions is at least as important as your actions.

> *Example:* Doug tells his companion he will no longer carry on a conversation while her attention is divided between the magazine and him. Is his motive to get her to put the paper down, or is his motive to simply send her a message indicating what he is or is not willing to do?

> *Caution:* His companion's thinking or interpreting his intentions to be controlling does not necessarily make them so. Only Doug can tell what his underlying intent is. By his actions alone, his intent could only be guessed.

The difference between the intent *to get* or *to give* is often subtle. Some emotional clues, however, can help. When your intent is *to give*, you usually feel calm and comfortable with what you are saying or doing. When your intent is *to get*, you usually feel agitated, frustrated, irritated, or afraid.

> *Key Point:* It is better to give than to get—you cannot always control what you get, but you can control what you give.

STEPS TO REMOVING THE BARRIER

1. When you are feeling frustrated or irritated with your companion, ask yourself what your intent or motive is for the conversation.

Ask yourself:

"Is my intent to give?"
or
"Is my intent to get?"

Notice the differences in the underlying intent in the following statements:

To Get	To Give
To get him to listen to reason	To give—or, to share—your thoughts or feelings
To get him to admit you are right	To give a statement of what you are willing or not willing to do
To get your point across	
To get him to understand	To give him opportunities to share his thoughts or feelings
To get him to show some emotion	
To get him to pay some attention	To give your attention
To get him to treat you kindly	To give understanding; To give love

2. During the next week, observe your motives or intentions as you think about wanting better communication. Notice how you act and feel when you are trying to get him to communicate better.

Key point: Even though your actions may be respectful, if your intent is to get him to change—as opposed to hoping he will change—you are out of line.

3. If he is reluctant to communicate at a particular time, remind yourself of an important rule:

> *Only talk when both of you want to talk.*

Reason: If you use a sledge hammer to get information out of him, you are apt to end up with a headache.

Better: Ask him "Is this a good time to talk?" Or "Do you want to talk?" If he doesn't answer, "Yes," don't push him—try again another time.

Important: Do not think for him. If he does not verbally tell you what he is thinking, do not try to analyze and figure out what is going on in his mind. Even if you usually guess right about what he is thinking, do not assume so until you know for sure. Do not speak for him. Until he is ready to make the effort to explain what he is thinking, do not take that responsibility away by speaking for him.

4. When your companion has a wall up, it is easy to get into a habit of analyzing, assuming, or guessing what is going on behind it—not to mention attempting to break through it. Rather than going through such taxing mental gymnastics, simply begin inviting him to come out from behind his wall. Some ways to invite:

• When you wish to discuss a sensitive topic, preface the discussion by explaining what you would like to discuss. Then, ask if he would be willing to discuss it. If he declines, at least you have given him something to think about. If he accepts, you have given him a choice and a chance to mentally prepare for a constructive conversation.

- Write a letter. Suggest that he may wish to respond with a letter, too. The reason for this is that some people are more comfortable with written correspondence than verbal communication. I suggest including three parts to a letter:

  1. Your appreciation for some of the things he does (or does not do).

  2. A few of your concerns about communication.

  3. Your hopes for finding ways to communicate better.

- Offer to meet with him for 30 to 45 minutes to discuss a mutually agreed upon topic within the Three Rules for Good Communication (Be Kind, Be Honest, and Have Constructive Intent). Offer to take him out to a movie and dinner with the money you save by not having to pay a marriage counselor.

  Caution: If he is not initially responsive, resist the tendency to give up or blast him. One husband approached his wife almost thirty times before they successfully discussed a particular topic. He showed a tremendous amount of self-discipline, respect, and patience. It finally paid off.

Making Excuses

COMMON INDICATORS

Thoughts: "He can't help it, because . . ."

Feelings: Overly patient, secretly resentful.

Actions: Ignoring or neglecting your own needs.

GENERAL INFORMATION

Having compassion for your companion's communication difficulties is highly commendable. If, however, you are making excuses for any behavior outside of the Three Rules for Good Communication or for his avoidance of communication, you are doing him a disservice. How is he going to have a chance to accept responsibility for how he communicates (or does not communicate) when you are making excuses for him? By providing excuses you are tempting him to think you are the problem and are somehow responsible for the solution.

STEPS TO REMOVING THE BARRIER

1. Think about the various reasons or excuses you give for his poor communication. Make a brief list of situations where you and your companion are having difficulties communicating. Next to each situation, write an excuse for his behavior.

2. During the next week, observe the thoughts that tend to go through your mind in response to his

undesirable behavior. Notice how quickly and creatively you can justify and excuse his behavior.

3. Try an experiment. For one week, whenever you start to think of an excuse, remind yourself he is responsible for his actions.

> Say to yourself:
>
> *"Regardless of my imperfections and life's challenges, he is responsible for his actions."*

4. Observe your reactions to the experiment.

Caution: Once you eliminate excuses and recognize his responsibility for his behavior, you may find yourself feeling more frustrated and resentful than before.

Solution: Focus your attention on what you can control—mainly yourself and your responses—rather than on his difficulties with communicating.

5. If he has not yet accepted responsibility for his behavior do not participate in a fruitless debate trying to get him to accept responsibility. Instead, respect his right to have his difficulties, even if he does not realize or admit them. Meanwhile, strive to live up to your standards for good communication.

Result: You will provide him with the best environment for objectively examining himself and, hopefully, reconsidering his view of how he communicates.

Blaming Yourself for Excessive Criticism

COMMON INDICATORS

Thoughts: "Something must be wrong with me."
"He will not talk to me or when he does, he is critical. I must have done something to cause this."

Feelings: Guilty, inadequate, confused.

Actions: Constantly trying to change yourself to satisfy him.

GENERAL INFORMATION

Your actions and imperfections are, of course, your responsibility. Even though your actions provide a positive or negative influence, his reactions to you, regardless of whether you are behaving reasonably or not, are first and foremost his responsibility—not yours. No matter how much you improve yourself, it is still up to him to decide whether he wishes to accept the responsibility of looking at himself objectively and making appropriate improvements.

Key point: The more you blame yourself or think that change on your part will cause him to change, the easier you make it for him to believe you are the problem and he has no part in it.

Common question: "How do I know if I am the problem or not?"

Answer: You can apply the "Rule of One Hundred." Imagine that one hundred reasonable people witnessed something you or your companion did.

Ask yourself:

> "Would one hundred reasonable people judge my behavior or his behavior as reasonable or unreasonable?"

Common question: "How do I know if I am behaving in a reasonable manner?"

Answer: Your responsibility is to communicate so that a reasonable person has a reasonable chance to understand. It is not your responsibility *to make* someone understand.

STEPS TO REMOVING THE BARRIER

1. Continue working to improve yourself in a reasonable manner, not because you are responsible for his actions but because you are responsible for your actions.

2. For one week observe how adept you are at blaming yourself and accepting responsibility for how he communicates (or does not communicate).

3. Frequently remind yourself of what you already know: Even if you corrected the main things he gets upset about, there would probably be other things to take their place.

4. When he reacts by refusing to talk or by talking in an unkind way, practice reminding yourself that his behavior (or misbehavior) is his responsibility—not yours.

> Say to yourself:
>
> *"His behavior is his choice and responsibility, not mine."*

5. When he behaves in an undesirable manner, do you take it personally by thinking: "He is doing it *to me*," or "He is doing it because *of me*"? It is better to simply remind yourself that "he is doing it" period!"

Example: When Diane had hurt feelings, Tom tended to become quiet and withdrawn. Diane thought, "Whenever I am upset, he will not talk to me."

Better: "Whenever I am upset, he becomes quiet and withdrawn." Notice how you feel and tend to act when you add the, "To me."

6. If your automatic reaction is to take his comments personally, practice developing a different response:

- Take several 3 x 5 cards and write something like:

> *"His undesirable behavior is simply that—undesirable—not a personal reflection on me."*

- Place the cards where only you can see them, at least a dozen times a day.

- Whenever you observe unreasonable criticism or avoidance of communication, whether his or someone else's, let your observation serve as a trigger to remind you of what is written on the cards. Say to yourself: "His undesirable behavior is simply that—undesirable—not a personal reflection on me."

Result: The more often he acts that way the sooner you will stop taking his actions personally.

Example: Tim was frequently angry about the money Dorothy spent on counseling. One evening, after his latest outburst, Dorothy responded differently. She calmly said, "One thing I got out of all the money I spent is that I now know you are not being rude *to me*. You are just being plain rude."

Caution: Usually it is better to keep this new insight to yourself, unless of course, you believe it would be helpful for him to know.

Basing Your Security or Happiness on Your Companion

COMMON INDICATORS

Thoughts: "How can I feel secure when he spends more time with work, church, or recreation than he does with me?"

"I cannot be happy unless he . . . "

Feelings: Insecure, easily upset.

Actions: Walking on eggs so as not to displease him. Nagging.

GENERAL INFORMATION

In a close personal or family relationship the natural inclination toward self-reliance can deteriorate. There can be a tendency for one or both parties to lean a little too much on the other. This can begin a slow, almost imperceptible, erosion of a healthy sense of independence and self-reliance. Without self-reliance, it is difficult to effectively communicate in an independent *and* intimate manner.

Example: Prior to marriage, Dawn was considerate of her family and friends' feelings; nevertheless, she made independent decisions based on what she thought was best. She was successful in several leadership positions at school and at church, where she demonstrated the ability to negotiate and make reasonable decisions even if everyone did not always agree. Yet in marriage she adopted the misguided notion that her happiness and security somehow depended more on her husband than upon herself. Peace at any price became her motto.

Result: She became overly hesitant to communicate clearly, and she avoided taking any firm stands. Her ability to confidently discuss issues and to contribute to making mutually agreeable decisions became paralyzed.

Key point: Like two pillars, independently yet jointly supporting a bridge, a healthy relationship is likewise supported by two independent, self-reliant people.

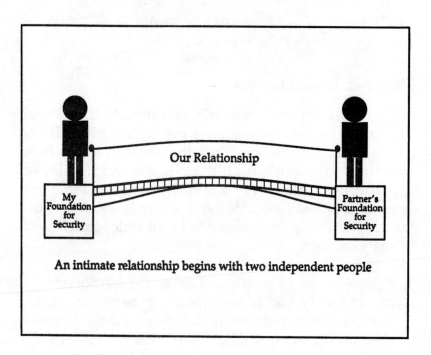

An intimate relationship begins with two independent people

STEPS TO REMOVING THE BARRIER

1. Ask yourself which is more important: good communication with your companion or managing yourself in a healthy, well-balanced manner. Obviously both are important, but if you put communication ahead of taking care of yourself, you will inadvertently create a barrier to better communication.

2. Think of a time in your life when you were particularly independent and self-reliant. You might even write a brief description of a poignant event during that time in your life. For the next month, review and try to relive that event for a few minutes, three times a day. This will encourage you to stand up straight and not lose your balance when he gets off balance or withdrawn.

   Result: As you become more independent and self-reliant, like a pillar of a bridge, you will be in a better position to promote good communication.

3. Whenever you observe your companion behaving in a way you do not like, remind yourself that your first priority is to manage your own life in a well-balanced and reasonable way. Although managing yourself better will not cause your companion to communicate better, you will begin to feel better about yourself and create an environment more conducive to good communication.

4. When you are frustrated by the lack of good communication, A.C.T.:

   (1) Acknowledge your feelings and the facts of the situation ("I am feeling frustrated" and

"It is the way it is: he is unable or unwilling to communicate any better for the time being.")

(2) Consider the available choices. Broaden your range of activities, develop more friends, take a class, exercise, read a book, develop a hobby, or get involved in church or community activities so you are not so dependent on your companion for happiness.

(3) Take constructive action.

Caution: If he decides to communicate better (and hopefully he will), be prepared to reevaluate your schedule of activities to provide enough time to work on improving communication.

Not Knowing How to Proceed with a Companion Who Will Not Cooperate

COMMON INDICATORS

Thoughts: "No matter what I do, he won't respond. So what do I do now?"

Feelings: Trapped, frustrated.

Actions: Fighting, withdrawing, or continuing as usual.

GENERAL INFORMATION

Sometimes, even after removing the barriers that get in the way of communicating better, a companion does not seem to be making any progress. While remembering it is his choice to work toward better communication or not, you can still do some things to increase the chances of him reconsidering.

Key Point: Make sure any steps you take are free from any intent to control or get others to communicate better. I cannot emphasize enough the importance of this. The recommended steps are intended to help you maintain your integrity and allow you to kindly and firmly exercise your right to only communicate within the rules you have set—*not* force others to change. However, it is all right, to hope others will respond in a cooperative manner.

STEPS TO REMOVING THE BARRIER

1. Write your companion a letter—again, if you have already done so—including:

   • What you appreciate about him.
   • Your concerns about developing and implementing some mutually agreed upon rules for communication.
   • Your hopes for better communication.
   • An invitation to respond in any way he prefers (in a letter, in person, or over the phone).

2. If, after patient, respectful and persistent efforts, he still seems unwilling to discuss and agree on rules for effective communication, you have an important decision to make:

   • First, to continue participating, whether actively or passively, in conversations where one or both of you are acting outside of your rules.

     Result: Possible illusion of harmony despite unsatisfactory communication.

   • Or second, only participate in conversations where both of you are adhering to the rules you have set.

     Result: Probably less communication with some disharmony to begin with until new habits are developed.

     Common Concern: "If I stick to my guidelines, we will hardly ever talk."

Answer: It is much better, at first, to talk successfully less often than to continue talking ineffectively more often.

3. If your companion repeatedly violates one or more of your guidelines, even after you have asked him not to, it may be necessary to take some practical, though possibly unpleasant and unpopular steps.

Common Question: "How do you deal with a companion persisting in unreasonable behavior?"

Answer: The answer is simple but surprising: "You do not." To attempt to reason with someone who is being unreasonable—is unreasonable. To even sit passively while your companion continues to act unreasonably is like applauding bad behavior. You unwittingly encourage it.

THREE STEPS FOR *NOT* DEALING WITH UNREASONABLE BEHAVIOR

Step 1: Kindly make a true, objective statement.

Example: "Ted, for the last three minutes you have blamed me for your unhappiness, told me I was incompetent as a person and as a wife, and have done so loudly enough for our neighbors to hear. I will not sit here and listen to this for one more minute.

If his response is reasonable, good communication could, perhaps, proceed. Otherwise, go on to Step 2.

Step 2: Politely end the "conversation."

Key Point: Say something kind before you postpone the conversation.

Example: "Ted, I love you and want to finish our discussion at a later time when we are both able to talk in a more respectful manner." Do not be surprised if he does not appreciate your polite exit, but at least you lived up to your standards. Even if he accuses you of running away or causing the communication problems "because you are so . . . ," do not take the bait and get hooked. If you do, you will be promoting the very thing you object to by communicating outside of your own rules for good communication.

Key Point: When arguing has become a habit in a relationship, ceasing to argue creates a temporary void. Strive to fill the void by doing positive things (leaving a loving note on the car seat, taking a walk, or going out for ice cream).

Step 3: Follow up later on the postponed discussion. Whether within a week, several days, or a few hours, kindly approach your companion and let him know of your desire to politely discuss and resolve the previously postponed discussion.

Example: "Linda, I know things didn't go so well when we tried to talk about . . . , but I would like to try again when you are willing."

Sometimes, at first, it is easier to write a

little note or talk over the phone, rather than talk face-to-face.

Caution: If your intent or motive in taking any of these steps is to *make* your companion communicate better, you are out of line. A more constructive purpose is to exercise your right to set and live up to your guidelines or standards for good communication and to give your companion the opportunity to do so or not to do so—hoping, of course, he will.

SUCCESS STORY

Lila loved her husband very much but was saddened and frustrated because they rarely talked. They could talk about superficial things but not about things that really mattered without Brent getting upset. She said he was a good man but somewhat insensitive to her feelings. Often Brent saw Lila as too emotional. He had no problem communicating as an executive who managed complex international negotiations for a large Silicon Valley corporation. But no matter how hard he tried, he could not seem to understand his wife's feelings. She would become frustrated and get down on herself or come on too strong with him.

Lila told me Brent was not willing to come in for counseling since he sincerely believed he was an expert in communication. Besides, he believed *she* was the one who had the problem anyway. "How have you been able to put up with such a lack of communication for so many years?" I asked. Lila explained that at first she thought his lack of communication was due to the stress of a new job. Then, as the children came along, she thought perhaps the strain of family life was a little too much for Brent. She just kept hoping things would get better—but they did not.

HESITATING TO TAKE A STAND

"Do you have the right to expect better, more personal communication from your husband?" I asked. She hemmed and hawed and finally said, "Yes, but I can't stand it when he gets so mad at me." She was more concerned about avoiding his wrath than taking concrete steps to promote better communication. I suggested that we did not want to intentionally upset him. However, if he easily got upset when asked to do something with which he was uncomfortable, she might expect him to feel upset when she asked him to communicate better at home.

I could see Lila had very little practice asking Brent to do something he might feel uncomfortable doing. I explained she had not given her husband a fair chance to deal with his discomfort and decide, perhaps, that he might want to learn to communicate as effectively at home as he does at work. She would not even allow him a good, healthy week or two to get beyond feeling upset before she would go back to reluctantly accepting things as they were. Sometimes, after he had been upset for a few days, she would feel so guilty or anxious, she would try extra hard to please him so they could once again have a good feeling between them, even though the original problem was being pushed under the rug.

At other times Lila would get so frustrated with his lack of communication that she would unwittingly do things to get a reaction out of him even if it was a negative reaction. She might burn his steak, say something stupid, or argue unreasonably. Her manner of dealing with her frustration and disappointment only strengthened his belief that she was not nearly as rational as he was.

REGAINING SELF-RELIANCE

Before Lila could learn to stand firm in a kind and respectful manner, it was necessary to rediscover what she had forgotten about herself since her marriage (that she was a basically self-reliant and independent person). I asked her to repeatedly remind herself that although she wanted her husband to be happy, his happiness was not the foundation of her life. Within a couple of weeks she was ready to take action.

Lila was not sure, however, whether she was willing to risk experiencing some current disharmony in exchange for the possibility of better communication in the future. As we talked, it became clear she had traded her former sense of self-reliance and independence for the illusion of marital harmony. As long as she did not require a reasonable level of communication, Brent seemed content. She agonized over whether to take a stand or continue to tolerate a substandard relationship. Finally, Lila decided it was unhealthy for Brent, the children, as well as herself, to continue pretending all was well.

TAKING A FIRM, LOVING STAND

Even before saying anything to Brent, some important changes were taking place in the way they communicated. Lila had drawn a line. She was no longer willing to accept the way they communicated (or did not communicate). She knew she did not have the right to try to make Brent change, but she did not have to put up with things the way they were. No longer would she pretend all was well or try so hard to get him to talk that she ended up looking like *she* had the problem. Brent was beginning to sense something was different. Her determination not to settle for less, despite her fears and anxieties, sent a new and clear signal to Brent that the current level of communication was unacceptable.

Next, she invited Brent out for a business lunch—a marital business lunch. She had three objectives for their meeting: (1) tell him how much she loved him; (2) share her concerns about the lack of quality in their communication; and (3) share her hopes for more frequent and personal conversations. The lunch went well, but after a few weeks Brent was back to being as critical or aloof as usual.

Lila wanted to know if there was anything else she could do. I reminded her of the importance of respecting Brent's right to not communicate better if that were, indeed, his choice. "There is more you can respectfully do if he continues to be unresponsive," I assured her. I warned her, however, when Brent realized she meant what she said about only talking with him when they both adhered to the Three Rules for Good Communication (Be Kind, Be Honest, and Have Constructive Intent), he might mistakenly think she was trying to control him or make him change.

I cautioned Lila, "If your intent is to make him change, you are out of line, and your attitude could contaminate and sabotage the otherwise constructive things you are doing." If, however, her intent was to strengthen the relationship, send Brent clear signals, and kindly stand up for what she believed in, she would be creating a healthy opportunity for change. She assured me her intentions were constructive and respectful of his rights.

I then gave Lila some specific actions to take, if, after kindly and lovingly doing everything else she could think of, he still did not cooperate. I suggested she: (1) let him know of her love, her concerns about their communication, and her hopes for a better relationship; (2) without becoming grumpy or aloof, cease joking, hugging, kissing, or otherwise doing things dishonestly suggesting she was satisfied with the relationship; (3) keep busy doing constructive activities, including something just for herself; and (4) verbally or in writing, regularly reaffirm her love for him and her commitment to the relationship.

RESPONDING TO THE CHANGES

It was difficult for Lila to remain strong *and* pleasant at the same time, but she worked very hard at it. Brent's initial response was to communicate even less. Then, after a few weeks, he became very upset as he incorrectly believed she was trying to change him. He said some cruel and upsetting things that in the past would have caused Lila to cave in. This time, fortunately for both of them, she did not take his comments personally, realizing he was having difficulty with the changes she was making.

After about two months of counseling with Lila, I was pleased to receive a call from Brent. I was impressed with his courage and humility. Here he was, a powerful executive who prided himself on being able to resolve even the most complex management and corporate negotiations, asking for help in communicating better with his wife. Brent told me that at first he thought Lila had a problem. Then after she began counseling he thought maybe the counselor had a problem. But, after awhile he realized that Lila was not trying to change him but was doing what she thought best for her and their relationship. She even seemed happier and more in control of herself.

Brent confided he had never felt comfortable dealing with emotions. As a child he had not been raised in a very open and warm family environment. He was taught to be responsible and work hard but not how to communicate intimately in a family setting—especially if there were differences of opinion accompanied by strong feelings. I found it especially easy to point out to him the principles of communication he had so effectively mastered in the business world, and then show him how to transfer those skills into his own home. We set some specific goals and laid out a plan of action he began to implement immediately.

WORKING TOGETHER AGAIN

Brent made great progress and within a month I suggested Lila join us to begin the final phase of the marital therapy. She was thrilled when Brent thanked her for sticking to her guns. He added that if she had not been so nice, he did not think he would have responded so well.

Then to further strengthen their marriage and communication skills, I suggested instead of continuing to see me, they arrange to hold a weekly Marital Council Meeting. The guidelines I gave them are included in the chart below.

Lila and Brent left excited and optimistic about using a weekly Marital Council Meeting to continue their progress in improving their communication skills.

In many relationships where there is a lack of communication, the problems can be successfully worked on and resolved without professional help. Even when only one companion is willing to acknowledge a problem, that person can, just by removing the barriers he has control over, dramatically increase the possibilities of developing a better relationship. If you kindly hold firm to what you believe is right, your partner usually (though not always) will respond—sooner or later.

Marital Council Meeting

❑ Meet for approximately thirty minutes, or as long as you both adhere to the Three Rules for Good Communication.

❑ Keep a record of what you discuss in a notebook, so you can refer to it at each subsequent meeting.

❑ Consider adopting a regular agenda where you discuss the following:

- *Appreciation*: Share what yo appreciate about your companion, especially during the last week.

- *Desired Improvements*: Share a few improvements you would like to make in yourself; then, courageously ask your companion for a few suggestions for you.

- *Planned Improvements*: Decide on one or two specific things each of you will strive to improve during the week. Perhaps you can have some fun by offering each other a back-rub, dinner out, or another treat as an incentive.

Summary

A brief summary of key principles and actions necessary to overcome communication difficulties is provided.

KEY PRINCIPLES

❑ Anyone can learn to communicate effectively.

❑ Thoughts and feelings do not change facts

❑ When two people adhere to the Three Rules for Good Communication (Be Kind, Be Honest, and Have Constructive Intent) they can discuss almost anything in a sensitive and productive manner.

❑ Any intent, let alone action, designed to control another person is disrespectful and unhealthy for the relationship.

❑ Making excuses for your companion or blaming yourself for his undesirable behavior only serves to support the behavior and increase the likelihood that it will continue.

❑ Like two pillars independently yet jointly supporting a bridge, a healthy relationship is likewise supported by two independent, self-reliant people.

❑ You do have the right to do what you think is right, regardless of what someone else may think.

❑ When you give 100% of your attention to the person you are talking with, you will think, feel, and communicate better. In addition, the other person will be apt to feel and appreciate your full attention.

❑ To attempt to reason with someone who is being unreasonable, is unreasonable.

KEY ACTIONS

❑ Determine your minimum standards or guidelines for good communication, including the Three Rules for Good Communication.

❑ Practice clearly labelling an opinion as an opinion, a feeling as a feeling, and a fact as a fact. When in doubt, ask yourself, "What are the facts that support this feeling?"

❑ With your companion, mutually agree on the rules within which you are both willing to participate in a conversation.

❑ Participate in a conversation only when you both agree to it and only when you are both acting within the rules previously agreed upon.

❑ In any given situation, especially when someone is upset, practice focusing on what you can control versus what you cannot control.

❑ Monitor the percent of attention you are giving to the person you are conversing with on a scale of 0 to 100 percent. Strive to give all of your attention whenever possible.

❑ When talking with someone, focus more on what you can give (your thoughts, feelings, and understanding) as opposed to what you would like to get (some common "get" positions are to "get" him to change his thoughts or feelings and "get" him to understand you).

❑ When your companion persists in unreasonable behavior, consider taking three steps: (1) kindly make a true, objective statement; (2) politely end the conversation by leaving; and (3) follow-up later on the postponed conversation.

❑ Consider holding a weekly *Marital Council Meeting* to discuss what you appreciate about each other, as well as the improvements you both desire in the relationship, and specific plans to improve.

Reminder: *Be sure to review the Central Principles section. Identify the principle(s) not effectively being utilized. Then take the appropriate steps to apply the principle(s).*

DEPRESSION

OVERVIEW

To think depression is something caused by factors beyond your control is downright depressing. Yet that is what many people believe, including some in the medical and mental health fields. Although in some cases medical problems do cause depression, the vast majority of depression is fortunately within your own control. If, however, after you try the suggestions in this book, you still feel depressed, I would encourage you to see a counselor or a physician.

Depression, like any other emotion, is usually the body's natural response to what is going on in the mind—whether consciously or unconsciously—as well as the body's response to how a person is eating, sleeping, and in general, living. Being in a world with so many unpleasant things such as illness, death, war, violent crime, hunger, broken homes, and homelessness, it can be difficult not to feel discouraged or depressed at times. Millions do everyday.

A LESSON ABOUT DEPRESSION

I learned more about depression from something my wife, Shelly, said to me than from all my school work and reading combined. I was in graduate school and we had just moved to Provo, Utah, to begin a very competitive doctoral program at Brigham Young University. We had been married for just two months and I started a job as a school counselor in a local district. I also received a Church leadership position. Soon feeling overwhelmed, I began to doubt my abilities as a husband, student, church leader, school counselor, and so forth. It did not take long for me to feel depressed.

For the first two days, Shelly did everything she could to encourage me and help me feel better. She even made my favorite dinners but to no avail. The next morning, she lovingly did something that taught me a great lesson. She asked if I was going to be depressed that night. Her question irritated me. She was implying I had some control over how I was feeling. Obviously, it was my circumstances, not me, that was causing me to feel depressed (or so I thought). I told her I did not know how I would be feeling in the evening.

I came home that night, after a long day at school and work, feeling pretty crummy. After another nice dinner, she asked me again, "Are you going to be depressed tonight?" I tried to explain as nicely as I could that I did not like the way I was feeling either, but I could not help it. She then gently indicated she would take care of her activities in another part of the house and leave me to myself (a rather unpleasant thought) until I was feeling better.

Even though I could not argue with her reasoning (I knew I was not very good company), I still felt hurt and a little resentful. But something happened to me. I began to review my options: Stay depressed and my wife does not want to be around me, or somehow climb out of my pit of depression and once again enjoy the company of my wife. It was as if a light turned on. Somewhere in the unconscious resources of the mind, solutions began to come to me. I could see light at the end of the tunnel and although I did not suddenly feel great, I was beginning to feel better. Shelly was surprised to see me so soon, when I went and gave her a big hug.

POWER OVER DEPRESSION

Despite being in a doctoral program studying about emotional problems and solutions, I fell prey to the popular myth that you can be rendered helpless against depression. Fortunately, I was given the opportunity to learn that you can have more power over depression than is popularly believed. Over the years, I have seen hundreds of people choose to become free from the grasp of depression after having believed circumstances or chemicals beyond their control were responsible.

Barriers to Overcoming Depression

There are ten common barriers that interfere with successfully dealing with depression. By identifying and removing the barriers getting in your way, you will be in a better position to minimize, and eventually control, depression.

Barrier 1: Self-defeating goals

Barrier 2: Depressed about feeling depressed

Barrier 3: Difficulty distinguishing thoughts and feelings from facts

Barrier 4: Exaggerated thinking

Barrier 5: Believing life *should* be . . .

Barrier 6: Difficulty distinguishing between what you can and cannot control

Barrier 7: Asking questionable questions

Barrier 8: Questionable nutritional, sleep, and exercise habits

Barrier 9: Shaky self-esteem

Barrier 10: Trying too hard to help others

Self-defeating Goals

COMMON INDICATORS

Thoughts: "I am going to get rid of these feelings."
"I am never going to feel that depressed again."

Feelings: Frustration, discouragement, short-lived optimism.

Actions: Lots of self-analysis. Looking for a quick fix.

GENERAL INFORMATION

Some goals encourage success while other goals interfere with progress, even leading to unintentional failure. No matter how well you succeed in fulfilling some goals, the desired result may still not be achieved. For example, you can obtain a good income but still not feel very secure.

Two of the most common and natural goals are to *feel* good and to *do* good. Unfortunately, these two goals are often in conflict with each other. Sometimes you may be doing something you consider to be "good," (getting out of bed in the morning, obeying the speed limits, or fulfilling an unpleasant responsibility) while at the same time not feeling good. Or you may be doing something that feels good that you do not consider to be good (turning the alarm off and going back to sleep, having a second helping of desert, or yelling at an inconsiderate driver). Fortunately, there are also occasions without conflict when you are doing something you consider "good," and at the same time, feeling good.

Rather than trying so hard to feel good, it is better—and generally feels better—to focus on *doing* good things. The goal of *doing* good things is solid, clear, and manageable. The benefits are two-fold: first, you accomplish something tangible, and second, you feel good about what you accomplished. If you fail to accomplish a worthwhile thing, you may feel badly about *it*, but you can still know your worth as a person is just as solid as ever. The security of that knowledge allows you to be more objective and patient with yourself and others.

The happiest and most successful people, therefore, set a higher priority on *doing* good than on *feeling* good. They place about 90% of their attention and effort on doing good and only about 10% on feeling good. Not that they do not enjoy feeling good—everyone wants to feel good—but they have discovered the important irony of feeling good: feeling good is more the by-product of doing good than the product of *trying* to feel good.

When you place greater emphasis on feeling good than on doing good, there is a natural, though counter-productive, tendency to try to directly control emotion. The "feeling" goal of trying to control or eliminate certain feelings, for example, usually results in more intense feelings. Like the flu, depression does not subside any faster by dwelling on it. In fact, the more you think about feeling crummy, the worse you usually feel.

Turning inward and focusing on pain, whether physical or emotional—although the natural thing to do—usually makes you feel worse. Instead, set goals to do specific things. "Doing" goals such as learning a skill, getting a job, cleaning a room, or calling a friend are not only more likely to be accomplished, they frequently result in better feelings. The *process* of accomplishing "doing" goals, however, does not always feel good.

When you are struggling with feeling depressed, for example, and set the goal "to not feel depressed," several

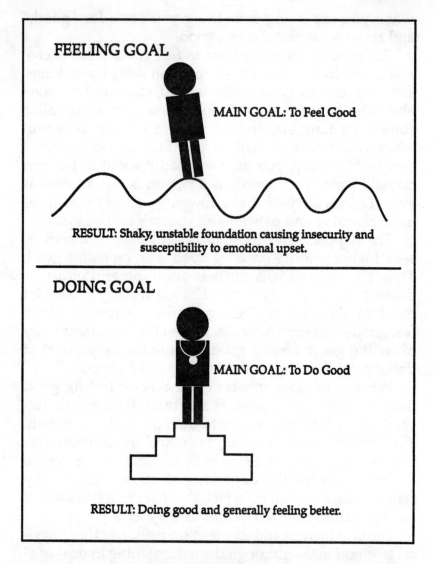

FEELING GOAL

MAIN GOAL: To Feel Good

RESULT: Shaky, unstable foundation causing insecurity and susceptibility to emotional upset.

DOING GOAL

MAIN GOAL: To Do Good

RESULT: Doing good and generally feeling better.

surprising problems begin. First, the more you think about *not* feeling depressed, the more depressed you are apt to feel about feeling depressed. Second, the more you dwell on your feelings, the less energy you have available for thinking about and doing something constructive. Third, since emotion is constantly in motion, as well as a highly subjective experience, accurate and objective measurement is difficult.

Barbara, for example, suffered a great deal of depression for several years and never saw herself making any progress, despite consistent and sincere effort. The first time Barbara came to my office she told me of her problem and disappointing lack of progress. She was excited about the suggestions and homework assignments I gave her and left with increased hope and confidence.

She returned a week later, noticeably less depressed, only to announce she had failed once again. Rather than focusing on her feelings, I asked her what she did on her homework. She reported significant progress and success on her assignments. Then why did she feel she failed? Her criteria for success was whether or not she still *felt at all* depressed. Since she still felt some degree of depression, she thought—and therefore felt—she had failed.

My criteria for her success was whether or not she improved her thinking and behavior. Since she did improve in those areas, I thought—and therefore felt—she had succeeded. Because she based her measure of success on the fickle ups and downs of feeling, she failed to notice the many times she was on the road to success. As she shifted her emphasis more to doing than to feeling, she not only did much better, she soon began to feel better.

STEPS TO REMOVING THE BARRIER

1. Notice if your reaction to feeling depressed is to escape!

   Problem: The attempt to escape from unpleasant feelings usually creates additional difficulties as well as compounds the initial feelings. Consider whether you use any of the common, though counterproductive, methods of escape listed on the next page.

Counterproductive Methods of Escape

- Eating
- Sleeping
- Drinking
- Using drugs
- Ignoring feelings

- Analyzing feelings
- Avoiding responsibility
- Withdrawing from people
- Trying to force the feeling to go away

---

2. Although you may be more accustomed to remembering times you felt depressed, there are just as many times you have come through the storm of depression to a beautiful, clear day. How did you do it? Think about it!

Example: Carl had a tendency to feel depressed—usually for one to three days—when life seemed particularly stressful or difficult to him. He was convinced he did not have any way to prevent or escape from the feelings of depression. After he gave me a few examples of times he felt down, I asked him how many times he would guess he felt depressed in his life. He said there were too many to count, but at least several hundred times, if not a lot more.

I told him I was amazed. "You mean," I said, "You have climbed out of the pit of depression several hundred times in your life. You are really good at getting out of feeling depressed. How do you do it?" He was shocked at first to consider such a perspective but then shortly began to discover he did have the power within himself to not only overcome depression, but to prevent it in many cases.

Result: By remembering and focusing on how

you climbed out of the pit of depression, you will identify successful principles and techniques that will be of great benefit to you.

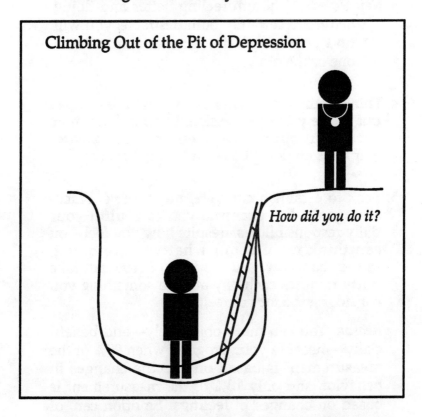

Climbing Out of the Pit of Depression

How did you do it?

Notice during the times you were climbing out of the pit of depression that you were doing two essential things: first, acknowledging to yourself the fact that you felt depressed, and second, continuing to actively participate in your usual activities, as well as striving to improve something in your life. Perhaps you were working at becoming better organized, accomplishing something you were procrastinating, or increasing your activity level.

3. Notice you generally have two desires or goals in response to feeling depressed:

- Feeling better.
- Doing better.

Key Point: Although feeling better and doing better are certainly both desirable, you will find yourself placing greater emphasis on one or the other.

4. Think again of the many times you have climbed out of the pit of depression. During those more successful efforts, were you placing greater emphasis on doing better or feeling better?

5. Seek to establish concrete, measurable, reachable goals. For example you can fulfill your daily responsibilities, despite how you feel. You can think more about what you are doing, rather than how you are feeling. You can take thirty minutes each day and do something you consider good for yourself.

Reason: You can more objectively—and beneficially—measure your progress when 90% of the measurement is based on specific changes in behavior, and only 10% of the measurement is based on changes in feelings. Emotion can, of course, be a useful catalyst to reevaluate performance, but it is usually not the most constructive criteria to use in measuring performance to begin with.

Key Point: Do not use feelings as the primary measure of performance.

6. Begin each day with a written list of "doing" goals—things you are going to do today, regardless of how you feel. Put at least six easy things on your list you would like to accomplish today.

Examples:

- Get out of bed at 6 a.m.
- Make the bed.
- Take a shower.
- Eat breakfast.
- Leave for work by 7:30.

As you complete each task, check it off your list. Even if you are not aware of feeling better right away, at least you know you are accomplishing some things.

Be patient! Feeling good often lags behind doing good. If you finish your list before the day is over, start a new list. By focusing on doing things, rather than feeling things, you not only see progress, but eventually you will begin to feel better.

Remember: By putting less energy into trying to analyze, control, or eliminate feelings, more energy is available for doing whatever you consider worthwhile, which will eventually lead you to feel better.

Key point: Goals that result eventually, if not immediately, in feeling better are usually "doing" goals, rather than "feeling" goals.

Depressed about Feeling Depressed

COMMON INDICATORS

Thoughts: "I must be pretty messed up to be feeling this way." "I shouldn't be feeling this way." "I hate feeling depressed."

Feelings: Lethargic, numb, stuck. Sinking deeper into depression.

Actions: Increasing withdrawal from people and activity. A lot of thinking and little action.

GENERAL INFORMATION

Depression is like emotional quicksand. The more you struggle and fight to get out of it, the deeper you sink. One reason you may get stuck feeling depressed is that you do not realize there are two levels or layers of depression.

Layer One: The initial feelings of depression everyone experiences from time to time. They last anywhere from a few minutes to a few hours. This level is like initially stepping into quicksand.

Layer Two: Depressed about feeling depressed. You sink to this level as a result of the understandable, though counterproductive, reaction of doing battle with your feelings.

Example: Brad, a successful attorney, had lost the zest for life he once enjoyed. He was going through the motions of living without feeling the emotion. He was successful at work but personally unhappy. For several months he balked at his wife's observations concerning him. He insisted he was fine. He was impeccably rational and certainly did not have any emotional problems. When he finally—and reluctantly—came to see me, it was readily apparent he considered himself too bright to be as miserable as he was. Not only was he initially embarrassed to feel the way the rest of us feel on occasion, he was severely condemning himself for feeling depressed.

Before he could begin making the personal improvements preliminary to feeling better, it was necessary for him to overcome depressing himself about feeling depressed.

Key Point: Before you can begin climbing out of the pit, it is necessary to first learn to acknowledge and give yourself permission to feel pure, unadulterated depression, without making things worse by fighting and resisting the unpleasant feelings.

STEPS TO REMOVING THE BARRIER

1. Notice what you say to yourself in response to feeling depressed.

   Depressing thought: I can't stand feeling this way.

   Better: I don't like feeling this way.

   Depressing thought: There's no reason for me to feel this way.

   Better: There is some reason, even if it isn't rational.

Depressing thought: What an idiot I am for feeling so depressed when I should be thankful for so much.

Better: You don't have to be an idiot to feel depressed—everybody feels that way sometimes.

2. Remind yourself that before you can start to make improvements necessary to feeling better, it is essential to first *acknowledge* and *accept* the temporary fact that you are feeling depressed. Say to yourself, "I am currently feeling depressed, despite my strongest and most sincere desires to the contrary. The unpleasant fact is, I'm not only feeling depressed about . . . , I'm also feeling depressed about feeling depressed."

Result: By repeating this statement over and over, you will more rapidly eliminate the second layer of feeling depressed.

3. If you are not yet finished being depressed about being depressed, give yourself some guidelines for dealing with feeling depressed. Set up a limited time and space to focus on depression. Decide on a special place you will go to think about feeling depressed such as the bathroom, an old chair, or a storage room. Give yourself a time limit, and strive to limit your depressing thoughts about depression to your special place and time.

Example: A friend of mine has what she calls a pity party. She invites herself and a large bag of M & M's to a secret party in her bedroom. Although normally conscious of health and fitness, she nevertheless has her special little party on occasions when she gets down on herself about feeling down. Then she gets going again, back on track, doing the kind of things she knows will eventually lead to feeling better.

Whenever she is tempted to feel sorry for herself, she just thinks of her pity-party, knowing she has already done enough of that.

Caution: Regular pity-parties with or without food are not conducive to good physical or mental health. Nor is a pity-party advised for severe or chronic depression.

4. Rather than viewing depression as an enemy, begin thinking of it as an irritating siren, warning you to take corrective action. Your challenge is to discover what that action is and then to take it.

   Key point: Depression, like physical pain or the making of mistakes, usually provides opportunity for learning and growth, albeit unpleasantly.

5. Seek to discover the meaning and potential value—not necessarily the cause—of the unpleasant feelings. Ask yourself, "How can I benefit from these feelings? Is the pain suggesting I do something differently? If so, what shall I do better?

6. If you are stuck feeling depressed about feeling depressed, be patient. Look forward to simply experiencing pure, unadulterated feelings of depression (just the initial feelings of depression) without depressing yourself about feeling depressed. Then you will be able to better get on with the business of doing something constructive, leading to feeling better.

Difficulty Distinguishing Thoughts and Feelings from Facts

COMMON INDICATORS

Thoughts: "I cannot be worthwhile if I do not feel worthwhile." "Since I do not feel love for my spouse, I must not love him." "I do not believe anybody loves me, so I guess no one does."

Feelings: Agitated over the conflict between feelings and facts.

Actions: Endlessly debating feelings versus facts. Arguing with those offering help.

GENERAL INFORMATION

When you are feeling depressed, your senses are dulled, even numb in some cases. The world is viewed through a dark and dreary lens, and things seem much, much worse than they really are. Life seems terribly cold and awful. At times like this—and we all have them—thoughts and feelings can be so strong that they are often mistakenly considered as facts.

Example: Jeff and Becky were having trouble making ends meet. For each of the last three months, their expenses were a considerable amount greater than their income. Rather than dealing with the facts—there were several ways they could earn more money as well as reduce spending—Jeff dwelt on his feelings of doom and gloom until he was convinced his feelings represented reality and, therefore, they were truly on the verge of bankruptcy.

Before feelings of depression will pass, it is absolutely essential to perceive the facts accurately, clearly distinguishing them from associated thoughts and feelings.

STEPS TO REMOVING THE BARRIER

Please see Central Principle 3: "Feelings versus Facts," page 40.

Exaggerated Thinking

COMMON INDICATORS

Thoughts: "This is absolutely terrible and awful."
"I cannot stand it." "I'll never feel better
again." "I am always making mistakes."
"Life is one crisis after another."

Feelings: Exaggerated. More intense than is necessary.

Actions: Extreme. Doing things for immediate
relief or escape, without regard to reason or future consequences.

GENERAL INFORMATION

On almost every occasion when you feel upset,
whether you are depressed or not, there is some form of
exaggerated thinking taking place. If you habitually tell
yourself, for example, you must *always* or *never* do something you cannot possibly *always* or *never* do, you have
set the stage for an upsetting play. Or when you think of
an event as *terrible, awful,* or *catastrophic*, rather than as
unpleasant or *inconvenient,* the emotional escalation is apt
to increase along the lines of your overly dramatic
"Hollywood" movie. Likewise, if you take a lopsided
and inaccurate inventory of your strengths, weaknesses,
and potential, your feelings about yourself will be lopsided and inaccurate.

Key point: The natural result of exaggerated thinking is exaggerated feelings.

STEPS TO REMOVING THE BARRIERS

1. Take several 3x5 cards and make and post signs to remind yourself:

> *Exaggerated thinking leads to exaggerated feelings*

2. Watch your language for any upsetting absolutes such as "must," "always," "never," or "can't." Substitute more objective phrases such as "It would be better," "I prefer," "I will," "I will not," or "I can."

Examples:

Upsetting absolutes: "I am always unhappy" (or "I am never happy").

More objective: "I am not often as happy as I would prefer."

Upsetting absolute: "I never do anything right."

More objective: "I do not do everything right, but I do some things right."

Upsetting absolutes: "I can't stop feeling so depressed."

More objective: "I can learn to feel better than I do right now."

Caution: Absolute language may be appropriately used in reference to the laws of God, nature, or man (To develop a close relationship with the Lord, a person *must* have faith; to maintain a driver's license certain

laws *must* be obeyed; a person who consistently violates the laws of health and nutrition *cannot* have a healthy body).

3. Notice the adjectives you use to describe
   unpleasant events in your life. Watch to see if
   you label events as terrible, awful, or catastrophic, rather than simply as inconvenient,
   unpleasant, or undesirable.

Examples:

Ray, a dedicated businessman, often complained of current or impending crises at work.
I explained that it was his choice whether he
thought of his work as a crisis or simply as a
challenge. A physician or fireman, for example,
after responding to several emergencies, usually does not think in terms of having to deal
with terrible, awful crises. Instead, he simply
thinks and talks in terms of doing his job, some
days being more demanding and stressful than
others.

Marissa was sick with the flu. At first, she told
herself she could not stand feeling so terrible
and awful. She discovered the result of such
thinking was to make her feel sick about feeling
sick. She then decided to simply think of herself
as feeling sick, telling herself that in time, the
unpleasant symptoms would surely pass. As a
result, she just plain felt sick, not anxious and
depressed as well.

The loss of a loved one—whether through
death or some other form of separation—may
be thought of as the end of the world or as sad,
undesirable, inconvenient, and survivable.

4. Notice how you feel when you use exaggerated versus moderate adjectives or labels.

Key Point: Because 85% of mental activity is automatic or unconscious, you may discover yourself upset or depressed before you are consciously aware of any exaggerated thinking. In such cases, you have probably developed a habitual tape or program of exaggerated thinking that automatically plays in certain circumstances. Even if you are not aware of the specific words, you can guess what they might be, based on how upset you feel.

Example: Virginia tended to feel depressed when Steve criticized her, no matter how gently he spoke. I asked her what she imagined when he attempted to discuss something about her or their relationship that he was uncomfortable with. She replied, "Oh, I feel he hates me and wishes he married his high school sweetheart. I worry that if I do not change, he'll leave me for a more desirable woman. Just about everyone is better than me." I told Virginia that she would make an outstanding Hollywood producer. She had taken a few simple facts and blown them up in her mind, making a melodramatic soap opera.

5. Practice substituting moderate and objective words in place of the exaggerated words.

Remember: For every second your mind is engaged in exaggerated thinking, volatile chemicals are dumped into your stream of emotion, causing increasing amounts of emotional turbulence. So the longer the exaggerated thinking takes place—whether consciously or unconsciously—the longer it will take to feel better.

6. To rapidly change a habit of using particular words, play a little game. First, make a list of upsetting absolutes or exaggerated words you are in the habit of using, along with a preferred list of more objective words. Whenever you catch yourself using an undesirable word, substitute a better word and give yourself one point. Whenever you catch yourself initially using a better word—give yourself two points. Compare your daily score against your previous best score. You can also offer a family member twenty-five cents each time he catches you using certain words.

7. Put your concerns in a more objective perspective by taking a piece of paper and drawing three columns and labeling them, "Desirable," "Undesirable," and "Terrible/Catastrophic." List some of the factual, current events in your life, placing them in the appropriate column. Be sure to record each event objectively, like a camera, with only the facts: do not give opinions, feelings or commentary. Do not forget to include things about your life that are objectively desirable, even though you may not feel that way right now.

Remember: How you decide to think about an event—not the nature of the event itself—determines in which column it is placed.

Key Point: The fewer things you *choose* to put in the Terrible/Catastrophic category, the less likely you are to feel depressed.

Example: A close friend of mine—a wonderful, healthy father of five—was diagnosed as having a malignant melanoma. He was given less than a year to live. At times he certainly felt his situation was terrible and horrible, but he decided he could live out his remaining days more happily and successfully by viewing his illness as undesirable and unpleasant. After the biopsy he and his wife did a surprising thing: they took a vacation and had a great time. He died shortly thereafter.

Current Events in My Life		
Desirable	Undesirable	Terrible/Awful/ Catastrophic*

*You do not *have to* put anything in the Terrible/Awful/Catastrophic column.

8. Avoid using intense, psychological words when describing how you feel (depressed, disturbed, manic, etc.). *Better:* Use more common and low-key words, such as "I feel down, low, or overly excited."

9. Examine your personal accounting procedure to see if you are being objective and accurate in recording your assets and liabilities. Develop a personal balance sheet—like an accountant does for a business—that will allow you to look at your life objectively.

Take a piece of paper and create three sections: Strengths, Weaknesses, and Potential. In each section, record your personal characteristics, attributes, skills, knowledge, and experience, being careful to use moderate, objective language.

Strengths	Weaknesses	Potential

Remember: You are recording objective facts, *not* your feelings. Just the facts, ma'am!

Key Point: Make sure the number of things in the Strength and Potential categories equal or, hopefully, exceed, those in the Weakness category. If you have trouble honestly finding positive things to list about yourself, imagine what your loved ones or best friends would say about you.

10. If you have a tendency to view yourself in a negative way, keep a daily log of your activities and accomplishments.

Key Point: Be sure to list the seemingly little things you do, but take for granted, like getting out of bed, getting dressed, having breakfast, putting things away, helping others, making phones calls, doing daily domestic or professional chores. At the end of the day, review and acknowledge what you have done, even if you feel like "I haven't done much of anything today."

Believing Life Should Be . . .

COMMON INDICATORS

Thoughts: "Life should be . . . but it isn't." "Why is life so hard? It is just not fair."

Feelings: Fluctuating between anger and depression.

Actions: A lot of complaining. Withdrawing from, or rebelling against, people or things.

GENERAL INFORMATION

In life there are positives, negatives, and always the potential for things to get better or worse. There is indeed opposition in all things. When some aspects of life (such as your feelings, relationships, or circumstances) are undesirable, thinking that reality *should* be different puts you in conflict with it. Fighting reality by demanding something be or not be so, is one of the more common causes of depression. Rather than focusing on finding ways to improve the situation—or your response to the situation—you end up struggling against reality, which results in anger or depression.

You may, nevertheless, be in the habit of thinking life *shouldn't* be the way it is. Many people habitually demand that life should be "fair," as they define fair. They seem to have a love of fair—to their own detriment and depression. Although everyone would like life to be fair, the fact remains, *life is not always fair.* Accepting this fact of life frees you to deal with life in a realistic and healthy manner.

Myth: By acknowledging and accepting reality as it is, you are condoning or passively accepting it.

Fact: By squarely facing up to the truth and facts of a situation, no matter how unpleasant, you are in a much better position to change the situation if possible, or if not, to control or change your response to it.

STEPS TO REMOVING THE BARRIER

1. Notice how you tend to respond to feelings or situations you consider undesirable. Watch for words or thoughts that fit your notion of how life should be against the reality of how it is.

Examples:

Life should be fair.

Reality: Sometimes it isn't.

I must get him to treat me nicely.

Reality: Sometimes you can't.

I've got to get out of this place.

Reality: You may need to stay for awhile.

I can't stand feeling this way.

Reality: You are feeling it anyway and you are standing it.

2. Common question: "What do you do when you do not like reality the way it is?" Answer: A.C.T.:

• Acknowledge the feelings and the facts as they

really are ("I feel the way I feel" and "It is the way it is"). Be careful not to damn up the stream of emotion by ignoring or fighting your feelings.

- Consider the available choices ("What are my choices? What shall I do, now?").

- Take constructive action.

To A.C.T. effectively there are three steps:

Step 1: Acknowledge.

To assist you to acknowledge reality as it is, rather than how you might be tempted to think it should be, view the situation like a video camera (taking in all the facts without any interpretation, editorial comment, or objection).

Practice distinguishing the "Camera Facts" from your personal thoughts and feelings. Take a piece of paper and draw a vertical line down the center. On the top of the left side, write "Camera Facts" and on the top of the right side, write "My Thoughts and Feelings." Consider a situation where you felt depressed. Under "Camera Facts," record the objective facts of the situation as a camera would record them. Be careful not to list your thoughts or feelings in this section. Under, "My Thoughts and Feelings," record just that, your thoughts and feelings.

Camera Facts	My Thoughts and Feelings
1.	
2.	1.
3.	2.
4.	3.
5.	4.
	5.

Result: By acknowledging reality (the facts of the situation and your feelings about those facts), you will be able to squarely face reality and consider the currently available choices.

Example: Valeen was depressed because she viewed herself as a worthless failure who could not make her husband happy. Rather than viewing the facts as a camera would record them—Darrel worked too much, ate too much, and did not get enough sleep—Valeen viewed his unhappiness as her fault and responsibility. When Valeen saw the reality that Darrell could not possibly be happy the way he was living, she realized how depressing and unnecessary it was to continue thinking she should somehow be able to make him happy.

Step Two: Consider your choices.

Consider the choices available and decide on your best choice.

Key Point: Even though the choice(s) you prefer may not be available, there are always choices available, although some more desirable than others.

Example: Although the choice to make Darrel happy was not available to Valeen, there were things she could do to make herself happier. She could also avoid making things worse for Darrel. Some of her positive options were to put her life and activities back in balance, pray for Darrel, do what she could reasonably do for him, avoid accepting responsibility for his feelings or reactions, etc.

Step Three: Take Action.

Do something constructive that will help you in the future: change any part of the situation that is changeable, change your attitude toward it, make the best of it, learn more about it and learn more about yourself.

Example: Valeen took the following actions: she stopped making unrealistic demands on herself, resumed doing the kind of things she did before she continued to care for Darrel, though she no longer carried his responsibilities. Even Darrel was relieved and pleased that she was no longer so unhappy about his unhappiness.

Key Point: Do not just sit around and think. ACT!

3. Identify words you tend to use that trap you into feeling depressed.

   Trap Words: • Should
                   • Have to
                   • Can't
                   • Must
                   • Never
                   • Always

   Notice how you feel when you use such words.

   Example: Deborah was so accustomed to using demanding "shoulds" on herself, she was easily upset or depressed. Her assignment for the week was to increase her awareness of how often she used "shoulds" and the resulting effect on her. She left my office determined to improve. In less than a minute she was back in my office laughing. While walking down the stairs she noticed herself beginning to feel tense. Then she realized what she was thinking: "This week I shouldn't use the word 'should.'" Be patient. Habits take time to change.

4. Identify words you tend to use that suggest you have a choice.

   Choice Words: • I prefer ...
                     • It would be better if ...
                     • I will ...
                     • I won't ...
                     • I don't like ...

5. Practice substituting Choice Words for Trap Words. As you begin using Choice Words, you

will be better able to deal with reality and less likely to feel depressed.

Caution: If you are currently feeling depressed, changing words is not likely to have much, if any, *immediate* impact on how you feel.

Difficulty Distinguishing Between What You Can and Cannot Control

COMMON INDICATORS

Thoughts: "I've got to get him to change, but I can't." "I have to do something, but I can't."

Feelings: Helpless, trapped, out of control.

Actions: Non-productive activity. Wasting time on less important activities.

GENERAL INFORMATION

Using mental and physical energy trying to control things or people that cannot really be controlled is equivalent to trying to blow up a balloon with a hole in it. No matter how hard you try, nothing happens: you just get tired. The brain does not automatically distinguish between what you can control versus what you cannot control. So if you are determined to control something you cannot in fact control, your mind will nevertheless keep searching for a solution—even though none is available. A mother who cares deeply for her children, for instance, may try so hard to help her children succeed, she dwells upon and worries about things she cannot control. This results a depressing drain on the brain, the body, and the relationship.

Myth: Caring means you are responsible for other's success and feelings. If you do not do what someone wants you to do it means you do not care.

Fact: A distinct difference exists between responsibly caring for someone and *carrying* their responsibilities. You may, in fact, care compassionately and responsibly, despite another's feelings to the contrary. *Remember*, just because someone thinks you do not care, their thoughts and feelings do not make it so.

Whether dealing with people or things, distinguishing what you can control from what you cannot control allows you to use your energy and resources in a healthy and productive manner.

STEPS TO REMOVING THE BARRIER

Please see Central Principle 4: "What You Can Control Versus What You Cannot Control," Page 48.

Asking Questionable Questions

COMMON INDICATORS

Thoughts: "Why . . . ?"

Feelings: Optimistic about a new answer/solution, only to be disappointed. Frustrated about not being able to find a satisfactory answer.

Actions: Endlessly searching for answers.

GENERAL INFORMATION

Questions, like goals, set the course your mind follows. Everyday we ask ourselves dozens of questions, with the answers determining our priorities and activities. From mundane questions such as, "What shall I have for breakfast?" to value-based questions such as, "Is it more important to stay at the office an extra hour or to go home?" Some questions lead to constructive action—often solving or preventing problems—while other questions create problems and interfere with solutions.

Example: I was the sixth therapist whom Doris consulted over the last ten years regarding her feelings of depression. She sobbed as she told me of the years of cruelty from her husband and the loneliness she had felt since her divorce. I asked her what she wanted to accomplish. She explained she needed some questions answered before she could overcome feeling depressed, namely, "Why am I feeling so depressed?" Thus far, ten years of therapy had failed to bring her answers and relief.

I responded by asking her whether she was more interested in finding out why she was feeling depressed or in finding out how to live a more satisfactory life. I explained that the question of "Why," was leading her on a speculative, theoretical, wild goose chase. Despite good intentions, her efforts were unwittingly creating barriers. Once she changed her question from "Why do I feel so bad?" to "How can I feel better?" her perspective changed. She then began to discover answers to her questions and the relief she was seeking.

The more time you spend searching for answers to upsetting or depressing questions—whether or not you find satisfactory answers—the more depressed you are apt to feel. By carefully evaluating the type of questions you are asking yourself, rather than automatically searching for answers, you will be able to identify and eliminate counterproductive questions.

STEPS TO REMOVING THE BARRIER

1. Examine the questions you are asking, whether to yourself or to others. Are they leading to answers that will help you progress? If not, cease asking such questions. Instead, Ask questions that lead to practical solutions and actions.

   Examples:

   Questionable question: Who am I?

   Better: What do I want to accomplish?

   Questionable question: Am I worthwhile?

   Better: What worthwhile things can I do?

Questionable question: "Does he love me?"

Better: Either ask him directly or drop the question.

Questionable question: "Why is life so difficult?"

Better: What are my options now? What shall I do?

2. Notice whether your questions focus on past, present, or future. Formula for success: 90% attention on the present, 10% on past or future.

3. Notice whether your questions focus on what you are doing or on what you are feeling. Formula for success: 90% attention on what you are doing, 10% attention on what you are feeling.

4. Consider how effectively you use the "Why" question ("Why am I feeling this way? Why is life so difficult?"). Does it lead you to do something constructive? If not, Ask yourself why you are asking yourself, "Why?" Some common reasons: It is easier to ask why than to take action, or it may be an unconscious way of complaining. If so, you can help yourself correct that habit by referring to the excessive use of "Why" as *"Whyning."*

Instead of asking "why," try asking yourself:

> "What are my options?" or,
> "What shall I do next?"

Key Point: Excessive self-analysis leads to paralysis.

Questionable Nutritional, Sleep, and Exercise Habits

COMMON INDICATORS

Thoughts: "I know I don't get enough . . ." "I know I need more . . ."

Feelings: Fatigue, irritability, or depression.

Actions: Maintaining undesirable habits or taking extreme measures to improve health.

GENERAL INFORMATION

When the body or mind is in a weakened state, you naturally tend to view life in a negative or exaggerated manner. It is unlikely for you to begin feeling better until you take better care of your body.

Example: Brett had been feeling depressed for several months, although he continued to work and fulfill basic responsibilities. He was getting about five hours of sleep a night, drinking about half a dozen caffeine beverages a day, skipping breakfast and lunch, and snacking daily on donuts and candy bars.

I suggested that he begin eating three meals a day, getting seven to eight hours of sleep a night, and dramatically decreasing his caffeine consumption, if not eliminating it entirely. I explained that until he began to take better care of his body, he was not likely to escape feeling depressed, no matter how many improvements he made in other areas of his life.

Key point: Depression is often an emotional warning signal, not an enemy to be crushed. It is usually suggesting you carefully examine yourself and make appropriate improvements.

STEPS TO REMOVING THE BARRIER

Please see Central Principle 8: "Physical Health," page 103.

Shaky Self-esteem

COMMON INDICATORS

Thoughts: "Who am I?" "Am I worthwhile?"

Feelings: Up and down like a roller coaster.

Actions: Seeking self-esteem through others, accomplishments, feelings, self-analysis, etc.

GENERAL INFORMATION

Please see Central Principle 5: "Self-worth," page 58.

Trying Too Hard to Help Others

COMMON INDICATORS

Thoughts: "I've got to do something to help him."
"I can't stand to see him so unhappy."
Feelings: Sympathy, frustration, resentment.
Actions: Unnaturally altering normal routine,
repeatedly talking about the same things,
etc.

GENERAL INFORMATION

When someone is hurting, it is only natural to want to help relieve the pain to whatever extent possible. If a person has a painful stomachache, for example, he can be given understanding and perhaps a little advice and encouragement, but not much else. Accepting the obvious limitations of how much help can be given is not difficult in such cases.

When someone is experiencing severe emotional pain, however, there is often a tendency to try to give more help than is possible or even helpful. Attempting to help a person do something he can only do for himself can create confusion over who is responsible for what. The "helper" often ends up carrying too much responsibility, while the person who could benefit from accepting full responsibility is actually weakened by retaining too little. Generally, the most beneficial thing to do is to genuinely believe in the other's ability to solve his own problem.

STEPS TO REMOVING THE BARRIER

1. When someone you care about is feeling depressed, think of what you can control versus what you cannot control.

   Result: Knowing the differences will allow you to put more energy into the appropriate areas so you can truly be of help. Draw a vertical line down the center of a piece of paper. On one side of the line, list what you can control, on the other side of the line, list what you cannot control. Example:

Can Control	Cannot Control
Expressing concern and understanding	His thoughts
	His feelings
Having faith and confidence in *his* ability to solve *his* problems.	His actions
Expecting him to continue acting in a responsible manner.	
Managing my own thoughts, feelings, and actions.	

2. Notice the intent or motive underlying your actions. Is your main purpose to give him the best possible environment and opportunity to progress or to get him to feel, think, and act better?

   Key point: You can control what you give in a relationship that may influence the other person, but you cannot control what he chooses to do—or what you get in return.

3. Practice showing respect for his right to feel upset, even if he believes he is not responsible for how he feels.

> Say to yourself:
>
> *"He does, after all, have the right to feel depressed, as well as the right to do something about it."*

Result: By giving what you can, rather than trying to do more and becoming a crutch, you give him the best opportunity to learn and progress.

4. You may be thinking, "But he doesn't have the right to make me miserable." That is true, and as you learn to do only what is reasonable for him—but no more than that—you will not be as entangled in his problem. He will be freer to find his solutions, though he may not feel so at first, and you will be free to go about your business (go into the other room to read, leave the house to go shopping, visit a friend and so forth).

5. Do not try to reason with him if he is talking or acting in an unreasonable way—to do so is unreasonable. Do positive and constructive things with him (take a walk, go see a movie, talk about uplifting things, etc.).

   Caution: Even talking about feeling upset in a reasonable way for more than a few minutes is rarely productive. It tends to prolong or intensify the depression.

6. If he wishes to discuss reasonable ideas and plans for self-improvement, proceed gently without rushing him toward a solution.

   Caution: Rarely give advice. Be careful not to

tread on his opportunity and right to progress in his own way and time.

7. Continue to live your life as normally as possible. Do not make major changes in your routine
such as reducing or eliminating your out-of-
home activities or staying by the phone in case
he calls).

8. Continue to expect (not force) him to perform
his usual responsibilities, despite how he feels.

Reason: Lowering your expectations or making
unusual allowances tends to convey a lack of
confidence in his abilities, inadvertently encouraging additional depression.

Key point: By caring for someone who is upset,
without carrying responsible for their happiness, you give them the best environment
and opportunity to climb out of their pit of
depression—without getting stuck in it
yourself.

SUCCESS STORY

The only reason Audrey came to my office was
because her husband strongly encouraged her to do so.
She came reluctantly. She was a very loving person who
spent many hours each day in service to her family,
church and community. Although she admitted she was
so depressed she could hardly continue to function, she
insisted she did not have time to be depressed because so
many people were depending on her. By keeping so busy
taking care of others, she had hidden her pain from just
about everyone—including herself. She politely, almost
desperately, pleaded with me to quickly do something to
relieve her of feeling so miserable.

It was obvious Audrey was so upset about being depressed, she had become "depressed about being depressed." Before she could begin to solve her problem it was necessary to remove the second layer of depression. I suggested she give herself permission to fully experience pure, unadulterated depression. She said, "That's ridiculous. I'm already doing that too well already." The fact was, she was trying so hard to ignore and cover up how she was feeling, she was stuck feeling depressed.

REMOVING THE SECOND LAYER OF DEPRESSION

Audrey was spending so much energy fighting the fact she was depressed, she did not have enough energy left to learn what could be done to put her life in better balance. She did not quite understand this line of thinking. She thought I was suggesting she stop acting responsibly, and instead, mope around looking miserable. I explained, "Your initial feelings of depression are like a person unintentionally stepping into a mud puddle. Your second layer of depression is like this person remaining in the mud puddle and stomping his feet up and down because he hates mud."

Depression is so unpleasant that it is understandable a person would not want to think about it. While some people magnify feeling depressed by dwelling on their pain, others find a way to cover it up. Some use food, alcohol, or drugs to mask the pain. Others spend an inordinate amount of time at work, away from their personal challenges. Audrey was doing something constructive— serving others—in part because she loved people but also as a way to ignore her pain.

In order to help Audrey first acknowledge and accept the fact that she was indeed feeling quite depressed, I asked her to do the following: "Go home and announce to your family you are feeling overloaded and depressed, and for two days you are going to do a little less than usual." At first, she balked, explaining she had to take care of her family. I told her if she would just rest up a little and stop telling herself she could not stand feeling depressed, she would then be able to get back to just dealing with the initial feelings of depression. As Audrey left my office that day she was upset at me for telling her to just feel depressed rather than "curing" her depression.

UTILIZING DEPRESSION TO MAKE IMPRESSIONS

When Audrey returned to my office a few days later, she looked a lot better. She said she finally understood what I meant. After a brief discussion it became apparent that her sense of identity and her self-esteem were tied up with service to others. Believing that she was not worthwhile unless she was taking care of others, Audrey inadvertently neglected taking care of herself. I suggested she could do more good, over the long run, if she also learned to take care of her own needs.

Audrey worked hard to make a few simple, but important, improvements in her life. Within a couple of weeks she developed a new attitude toward herself and others. She began an exercise class, learned to delegate, and began to occasionally say "No." Audrey continued to be very service-oriented—however, no longer at the price of neglecting herself. She became aware of her own self-worth and quickly became a much happier person.

Summary

A brief summary of key principles and actions necessary to overcome depression is provided.

KEY PRINCIPLES

- ❑ Attempting to ignore, control, fight, or eliminate the stream of emotions creates a dam that blocks the natural flow of emotion, thereby causing unpleasant feelings to grow in magnitude and intensity.

- ❑ Before you can start to make improvements necessary to feeling better, it is essential to first acknowledge and accept the fact of feeling depressed.

- ❑ Exaggerated thinking leads to exaggerated feelings.

- ❑ At any given moment life is the way it is, whether you think it should or shouldn't be.

- ❑ Depression is like an irritating siren—intended to help rather than hurt—warning you to take corrective action.

- ❑ When the body is not getting sufficient food, exercise, or rest, it is highly susceptible to feelings of depression—independent of any other circumstances or thoughts.

❏ There are two distinctly different, though related, aspects of self-esteem. First, there are natural, God-given aspects of self-esteem unique to each person. Then there are the fickle feelings of self-esteem which can change almost as suddenly as the weather.

KEY ACTIONS

❏ Focus more on *doing* better, than on *feeling* better.

❏ Avoid asking yourself why you feel depressed, unless asking leads you to action-oriented solutions.

A.C.T.:

❏ Acknowledge the feelings and the facts as they really are. Be careful not to dam up the stream of emotion by ignoring or fighting your feelings.

❏ Consider the available choices.

❏ Take constructive action based primarily on the facts rather than on the feelings.

❏ Replace exaggerated thinking with objective and moderate thinking

❏ Avoid using Trap Words: "should," "have to," "can't," "must," "never," "always," "no choice," etc. Instead, substitute Choice Words such as, "I prefer . . . ," "it would be better if . . . ," "I will . . . ," "I won't . . . ," "I don't like. . . ."

❏ Try an experiment. Decide on some manageable improvements you would like to make in your eating, sleeping, or exercise habits. Practice your improvements for thirty days, then see how much better you feel.

❏ When you come upon a problem (either face-to-face or in your mind), ask yourself:

> *"What aspects of this problem can I control versus what I can't control?"*

❏ When you notice yourself dwelling on things you can't control, ask yourself:

> *"Do I really want to be thinking about this?"*

❏ Then, practice thinking about or doing something you can control.

❏ Observe how you use the two most important words affecting your identity and self-esteem—I am."

Warning: Any use of these words to describe yourself in any other way than, for example, "I am 'Laurie," "I am a person," "I am a child of God," "I am a woman," may be hazardous to your self-esteem.

❏ Rather than attempting to describe who you are, describe what you think, feel, do, or have ("I have certain talents, accomplishments, relationships" or "I like to play the piano, jog, spend time with friends.")

Reminder: *Be sure to review the Central Principles section. Identify the principle(s) not effectively being utilized. Then take the appropriate steps to apply the principle(s).*

UNSATISFACTORY
INTIMACY

OVERVIEW

Sex is easy. It is instinctive and generally pleasurable for all living species. People throughout the world, for thousands of years and without the "benefit" of sex manuals or therapists, have successfully reproduced.

Your overall relationship with your spouse can be compared to a beautiful cake with sexual intimacy being the frosting on the cake. If after preparing the ingredients for a cake, you realize you are out of sugar, there are several options. You could go ahead and bake the cake anyway, later on trying to make up for the lack of sweetness by applying extra frosting. Although that might create the appearance of a great cake, it would lack in substance and satisfaction. Or, better yet, you could take the more time consuming and difficult course of *first* doing whatever it takes to provide *all* of the essential ingredients.

> *Key Point*: If a marriage is lacking an essential
> ingredient, focusing on sexual performance
> alone will not produce a satisfactory outcome.

Whereas sex is easy, developing a loving, intimate relationship based on respect, communication, unselfishness, self-control, etc., takes a powerful commitment and a lot of hard work and patience. As two people develop such a relationship, they find there are many intimate, personal ways to express their love. Sexual activity is just one such way to convey love.

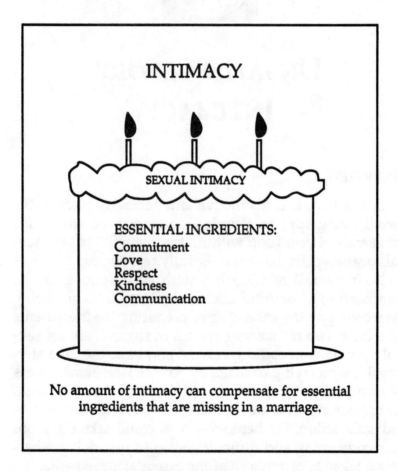

INTIMACY

SEXUAL INTIMACY

ESSENTIAL INGREDIENTS:
Commitment
Love
Respect
Kindness
Communication

No amount of intimacy can compensate for essential ingredients that are missing in a marriage.

INTIMACY IS MORE THAN SEX

Many people think of intimacy as mainly referring to sexual activity. Although intimacy may include sexual activity, intimacy itself is much larger and more important than sexual activity. Intimacy includes all the essential aspects of the relationship (love, respect, commitment, communication, kindness, unselfishness, emotional and physical closeness). Even the more physical part of intimacy includes many intimate aspects that are not sexual (sitting next to each other, giving a loving touch, holding hands, hugging, kissing, cuddling). Paradoxically, when sex takes on greater significance than other essential aspects of marriage, unsatisfactory intimacy is often the result.

Sex, without intimacy, is shallow and only briefly satisfying. When sex does not mean anything more than passing passion or physical pleasure, it tends to become progressively less satisfying. Some people become less interested, while others seek more sex or different types of stimulation in order to feel satisfied. Yet they find nothing but dissatisfaction.

> *Key point:* Overall intimacy is essential in order
> for sexual intimacy to be fully enjoyed.

When people experience sexual difficulties, they often incorrectly assume that the root of the difficulty is sexual. *Result:* Over-emphasis on one aspect of the relationship, excessive blame, self-doubt, frustration, resentment, and worst of all, overlooking the areas where the solutions are often found. The sexual difficulties of about 90% of the people who come to my office, for example, are resolved without focusing on the sexual problem itself. Instead, when couples focus on identifying and providing the essential ingredient(s) often lacking in the overall relationship, intimacy in general usually improves. In time, sexual intimacy becomes more enjoyable as well.

> *Key point:* By placing more importance and attention on improving the overall relationship, sexual intimacy naturally tends to improve.

COMMITMENT: FOUNDATION OF INTIMACY

The central feature of intimacy, whether it be sexual intimacy or not, is commitment. Commitment is another word for love. When two people make a commitment to each other, along with common goals, values, respect, and friendship they have the foundation for building a great relationship. The root of lasting, secure love is the commitment two people make to each other. Whereas the feelings of love rise and fall like the tide of the sea, commitment is like a solid rock basking in the sunshine, even withstanding the pounding of crashing waves.

> *Key point:* Feelings of love usually accompany commitment, but commitment does not necessarily accompany feelings of love.

Intimacy can be expressed and shared in a tender, meaningful and lasting manner without sex. I have seen a loving husband wheel his severely brain-damaged wife into church, tenderly holding her unresponsive hand throughout the entire meeting. I have seen a wife whose husband was rapidly failing with Alzheimer's disease, lovingly reminding him of his name. Such examples of intimacy, built over the years on a foundation of commitment and love are more solid than any emotion or passing passion could ever be.

The love and commitment a husband and wife have for each other can also be intimately expressed in a sexual way. Sexual intimacy, in addition to being the means of bringing children into the world, then becomes an important and enjoyable symbol of their commitment and love. As two people learn to become increasingly intimate in their overall relationship, not just in bed, their love will grow, as will their ability to enjoy a deeper and more lasting form of sexual intimacy.

Barriers to Resolving Unsatisfactory Intimacy

There are seven common barriers that can interfere with resolving unsatisfactory intimacy. By identifying and removing the barriers getting in your way, you will be in a better position to work toward achieving the quality of intimacy you desire.

Barrier 1: Lack of real or perceived commitment

Barrier 2: Trying to control emotion

Barrier 3: Fear of failure

Barrier 4: Attaching undue meaning to sexual activity or performance

Barrier 5: Missing ingredient(s) in the relationship

Barrier 6: Basing your security or happiness on your spouse

Barrier 7: Too busy, too tired, or just not interested in physical intimacy

Lack of Real or Perceived Commitment

COMMON INDICATORS

Thoughts: "Does he love me?" "He cares more about . . . than he cares about me."

Feelings: Anxious, insecure.

Actions: Spending less and less time doing positive things together.

GENERAL INFORMATION

If intimacy means that two people love each other and are committed and that one person's commitment is questionable, the meaning of sexual behavior can be confusing. One partner may be left wondering if sex means anything beyond the pleasure of the moment to the other partner. Confusion usually leads to misunderstanding and hurt feelings, creating an environment that is not conducive to intimacy.

Although sexual difficulty or dissatisfaction does not always suggest a lack of commitment, a lack of commitment is usually accompanied by sexual difficulty, if not in the beginning, then later on in the relationship.

Key point: A common underlying cause of sexual dissatisfaction is a real or perceived lack of commitment.

STEPS TO REMOVING THE BARRIER

1. Decide you are willing to honestly evaluate how

committed you are to your spouse, as compared to other relationships or activities. *Reason:* Some people are more committed than they think or communicate, while others are less committed. Only you can objectively and completely evaluate your degree of commitment.

Myth: Commitment means you are *irrevocably* trapped.

Fact: Entering into a commitment and remaining committed is a choice that you, and you alone, control.

2. List your priorities in life as they currently stand, not as you might think they *should* stand (self, God, marriage, work, etc.). A common mistake is forgetting to place yourself on your priority list.

   Key point: If you neglect your own personal welfare, even for the sake of your marriage, you will not be at your best.

3. Consider the following questions designed to assist you in evaluating how committed you are to your spouse:

   - Do you generally prefer to be with your spouse or with work, children, friends, recreation, yourself, etc.?
   - Do you consider your marriage to be your most important relationship, other than your relationship with the Lord and with yourself?
   - Do your actions suggest you are committed to your spouse?

   Myth: Commitment means you always feel loving toward your spouse and do what he wants you to do.

   Fact: Feelings, like the waves of the sea, are constantly rising and falling. A commitment is more than how you feel. The root of a commitment is a decision you make in your mind, that when acted upon bears fruit in the form of your actions. It is something special that is within you.

4. Reevaluate your priorities. Make sure you continue doing important nonmarital things, while at the same time, putting your marriage ahead of work, children, friends, recreation, T.V., hobbies, or anything else. Then, if needed, make the most powerful and important marital decision possible: decide to put your marriage first.

Trap: Trying to make your spouse believe you are committed. *Reason:* Like the root of a tree, your decision to be committed to your spouse is beneath the surface, within the private confines of your mind. It cannot be seen by another person with absolute certainty.

Avoid the trap: Let your actions, more than your words, be seen as the evidence or fruit of your commitment. Act out your commitment by spending quality time with your companion, keeping your word, even when it is inconvenient, etc.

Caution: If your spouse feels hurt or mistrust, it may take him weeks or months to see and taste the fruit of your commitment. Be patient.

Myth: Commitment means your spouse feels you are committed.

Fact: You and you alone—not anyone else—can determine if you are committed, and if so, to what extent. Ironically, your spouse may feel

you are committed, when in fact, you are not—
or vice versa.

5. Discuss with your spouse how committed you
   are to each other.

6. To reaffirm and strengthen your commitment:
   place your companion's picture where you can
   see it daily. Whenever you are involved with
   someone or something that once was, or could
   become, more important than your spouse,

> Say to yourself:
>
> *"My marriage is more impor-*
> *tant to me than . . ."*

Communicate your commitment by telling your
spouse daily, if possible, that you love him and
that he is more important to you than anyone or
anything else, even if he does not fully believe
you at first.

Discuss with your spouse the types of words
and behaviors that mean commitment and love
to both of you. A common mistake is that you
do something that means commitment to you
such as bringing home a paycheck or making a
meal, and your spouse does not attach the same
meaning to what you did. This results in misunderstanding and hurt feelings.

Caution: Participating in sexual intimacy prior
   to both of you being committed may interfere with the progress of the relationship,
   as well as cause unnecessary pain or sexual
   dissatisfaction, or both.

Trying to Control Emotion

COMMON INDICATORS

Thoughts: "A mature adult is one who controls his emotions."

"If I don't control my feelings, I may do something I'll regret."

Feelings: Afraid of being hurt, losing control, or doing something unreasonable. Feeling numb.

Actions: Appearing unusually calm, strong, quiet, stable, or unemotional. Rarely talking about feelings.

GENERAL INFORMATION

Nobody wants to feel frightened, insecure, or hurt—especially when it comes to intimacy. Rather than risk being hurt, some people—whether consciously or unconsciously—decide not to let themselves get close. In a misguided attempt to control emotion, some people become emotionally and sexually numb; others go through the physical motions of sex without feeling loving and intimate.

Paradoxically, the more you focus on your feelings or avoid them, the less able you are to enjoy intimacy. By permitting yourself to fully experience waves of emotion, whether pleasant or not, without any form of tampering, you are better able to learn to swim in the exciting and sometimes turbulent waters of love.

STEPS TO REMOVING THE BARRIER

1. Notice times you experienced emotion without trying to control it. Especially think of times with your spouse when you were not so concerned about controlling emotion or about losing control (maybe when you played tennis, kissed good-bye, hugged, or participated in an intimate conversation).

   Caution: This does not refer to times you were thinking irrationally or behaving irresponsibly. Such thoughts or behavior, obviously, invite your attention and self-control.

   Example: At a restaurant with your spouse, you allowed yourself to feel anticipation and excitement about the meal, or even disappointment or frustration, without being unduly hurt or acting irresponsibly. How did you do it? You probably did not think you were "losing control." Why not?

   Key point: When you feel good, you usually do not try to control your feelings (I am referring to your internal feelings here, not your external behavior). You have learned by experience that controlling the thoughts and behavior that bring about the good feelings, rather than trying to control the feelings themselves, allows you to generally feel better and for a longer period of time. (Too many people get into denial and stuff their feelings when they try to ignore, fight, or control how they feel.)

3. Try an experiment. The next time you are feeling really good, focus on how you are feeling

and try as hard as you can to control it. Try to hold on to the feeling so it does not escape you. Notice how *the* harder you try to directly control emotion, the worse you tend to feel.

4. Try another experiment. Select a time with your spouse when you can participate in some mutually agreeable sexual activity during which you tend to feel a little uncomfortable. In a gentle and loving way begin the activity. Instead of trying to control your emotions (trying to fight or change how you feel), monitor them on a scale of one to ten with ten being the most uncomfortable you have ever felt and one being the absence of any significant discomfort.

Notice how the feelings of discomfort tend to subside as you acknowledge, rather than fight them. Repeat the experiment on several occasions, if necessary, until you can accept rather than resist any uncomfortable feelings.

Caution: Since this is an emotional experiment, do not judge your sexual performance. Just observe your emotions and reactions.

5. For one week, whether during intimacy or your regular activities, rather than trying to control your emotions, try taking the following actions:

• Give yourself permission to fully experience your emotions whether pleasant or unpleasant.

> Say to yourself:
>
> *"It's more important to control my thoughts and actions than my emotions."*

- Acknowledge and accept the existence of your emotions as you would acknowledge fluctuations of your automobile's instruments.

- Use your emotions as a key to provide valuable information about yourself and ways you can improve.

- Share your feelings within the Three Rules for Good Communication (Be Kind, Be Honest, and Have Constructive Intent).

Fear of Failure

COMMON INDICATORS

Thoughts: "I've got to do it right this time. But what if I can't?"

Feelings: Anxiety, nervousness, fear, discouragement, depression, apathy.

Actions: Trying too hard or avoiding trying.

GENERAL INFORMATION

One of the greatest lectures on sexual difficulties was given by Franklin D. Roosevelt: "You have nothing to fear but fear itself." Fear of failure itself "interFEARS" with learning and enjoyment. Most people have more trouble being "at their best" when under pressure to perform. Even those who seem to do well under pressure do not usually handle intimacy very well if they are afraid of failing.

STEPS TO REMOVING THE BARRIER

1. Think of and discuss times when you were not afraid of failing (sexually or nonsexually). What was different about those times? Especially note what was different during the nonsexual times when you were relaxed and having a good time together.

2. Place the sexual difficulty, which may initially appear large and overwhelming, into a context

and perspective that will render it more manageable by taking the following actions:

> Ask yourself:
>
> *"Is the relationship itself or my sex-
> ual performance more important?"*

Key point: For a healthy, long-lasting relationship, it is essential that individuals consider their overall relationship as more important than any single aspect of the relationship.

• Whenever you think about intimacy not
going as well as you would like, remind
yourself and your partner that your love for
each other is more important than the present concern.

• Imagine that you or your spouse have a medical problem interfering with or preventing
sexual satisfaction. Would you still love him?
Discuss why you love each other through
storms of medical problems or even sexual
difficulties. When sex is not the most important part of the relationship, sexual difficulties are more readily resolved because they
are more of a discomfort or inconvenience
than a problem to be feared.

• Notice some of the things each of you do to
show the relationship is more important than
sexual performance. For example, you may
verbally reassure each other that this difficulty is small compared to your love and commitment to each other. You may also convey
your love by continuing to enjoy doing a
variety of things together, as well as simply

being kind and respectful to each other, even though sexual activity is not yet as good as you would like.

3. Redefine the meaning of success and failure in a way to encourage success and discourage the likelihood of failure, by taking the following actions:

- Divide success in intimacy into two categories—primary and secondary success:

    Primary Success: That which is essential for building a great relationship (love, commitment, giving and receiving nonsexual affection, willingness to work together to solve any marital difficulties).

    Secondary Success: That which is desirable, like the frosting on a cake, though less important than the cake itself (erection, orgasm, having the kinds of feelings during intimacy you prefer, etc.).

    Caution: Since secondary success cannot be as directly or immediately controlled as primary success, trying too hard to obtain secondary success actually interferes with achieving it.

- Draw a vertical line down the center of a piece of paper. Write Primary Success on the top of one side of the line and Secondary Success on the top of the other side. Privately consider factors pertaining to overall intimacy as well as sexual intimacy and place them in either the Primary or Secondary Success category.

- Before you share your paper with your spouse, agree with each other that although secondary success is important, primary success is even more important and will generally precede secondary success. Also, agree that failure will only occur when someone permanently gives up hope and stops trying. Then respectfully and honestly share and discuss your paper.

Key point: By placing primary success first, you build the foundation from which you can learn to achieve secondary success without the interference of fear.

- Practice focusing more of your attention and efforts on what you define as your primary success. As your primary successes increase in quantity and quality, there is greater likelihood of secondary success.

4. Utilize fear to help build a better and more loving relationship, by taking the following actions:

- Think about what you are specifically afraid of failing to achieve during intimacy (such as erection, orgasm, or having the kinds of feelings you prefer).

- Whenever you think of or experience something you used to fear, or consider a failure, connect it with something positive. For instance, if orgasm does not occur, give each other a reward for trying and for achieving some primary success.

Examples:

> Give a back rub, listen to some favorite
> music, spend time talking about some-
> thing light, plan a night out, etc.). *Result:*
> Instead of resisting the fear, inadvertently
> making things worse, you are using it to
> help strengthen your relationship.

• Notice and discuss how much love and effort
was shown by each person in the process of giving and receiving love, regardless of the results.
Afterwards, you can strengthen and reinforce
the foundation of the relationship by saying
something nice, giving a hug, or sending a little
note of thanks.

• Allow yourself to ride out the wave of fear,
knowing that in time it will pass. Meanwhile,
give each other extra consideration and reassurance. Do not fight or resist the fear.

Attaching Undue Meaning to Sexual Performance or Activity

COMMON INDICATORS

Thoughts: "Does he love me?" "If he loved me, he would..."

Feelings: Frequent or prolonged agitation concerning sexual activity.

Actions: Excessive avoidance of, or interest in, sexual activity.

GENERAL INFORMATION

In every healthy marriage, there are times when one person wants to be sexually intimate and the other is not interested. Just as your desire to go out to dinner may not always coincide with your spouse's desire to eat out, so it is with sexual desire. You may feel like going out one night, while he is not the least bit interested, or vice versa. You probably would not think, "If he loves me, he will feel like going out the same time I feel like going out." You would just think he does not feel like it tonight and not think any more about it.

Sometimes, however, it can be tempting to take "no" to intimacy as a personal rejection or statement about your personal worth, thinking "I must not be very desirable." Usually it means nothing of the sort. Often it simply means he is tired, preoccupied, stressed, or emotionally drained. Sometimes one person reacts to stress by desiring to be physically close, while the other responds by preferring to be alone. If you attach a meaning to his "no" that says you are not worthwhile or that he does not love you, you may be creating a problem that does not exist.

If your spouse feels pressure to make you feel worthwhile or loved by initiating sexual activity, he may lose his desire. Or he may sincerely try to please you, only to discover that no matter how hard he tries, you still feel down. He may then feel that he is failing—and consequently feel frustrated or inadequate. When you see his lack of desire or frustration, you may mistakenly think his feelings mean you are not worthwhile or loved. This creates a vicious, escalating cycle.

STEPS TO REMOVING THE BARRIER

1. Think of times when the lack of sexual intimacy did not significantly affect your feelings of worth, happiness, or love. What was different then? How did you do it?

   Example: Keith and Shauna often became embroiled in conflict when she said, "No." I asked them to think of a time when they did *not* have a problem with "no." At first, they could not think of any exceptions to their problem. Then they recalled one time.

   After a romantic night out, Keith had been looking forward with excited anticipation to being intimate with his wife. Just as he began to give her a passionate kiss, she said "Not tonight, dear." Then she added, "I love you and enjoyed our evening together. I just don't feel up to it now. How about a rain check?" Keith was disappointed to say the least. His natural reaction was to object, but this time he thought more of her than of himself. He did not want her to feel like it was the worst thing in the world that ever happened to him, so he did something unusual. He said, "Shauna, although I am disappointed, I too love you very much, and it's okay."

As we discussed that night, they began to discover some solutions to their problem.

2. Think about what sexual intimacy means to you. Does it mean "I love you" or does it just mean physical pleasure? Do you view it as the frosting on the marital cake or the cake itself? Is your love for each other communicated in many ways, with sexual intimacy just being one special way to express it? Or is sex the primary or only way of expressing love?

3. Gently invite your spouse to discuss the meanings both of you attach to intimacy. This will result in increased understanding which will create a more supportive environment for constructively dealing with any sexual difficulties.

   Key point: It is initially more important to understand and respect each other's way of thinking than it is to think the same way.

   Caution: Many people have never stopped to think about the meaning of sex, so be patient if it takes awhile to identify and share how you or your spouse feels.

4. Do not assume you know what your companion's behavior means, especially when there is some difficulty, unless he has clearly explained it to you. It would be better to say to yourself, "I don't know what this means." Then, if you are still interested, ask your spouse. You might say

something like, "I love you very much and
would like to know what our current sexual situation means."

5. Each time you discuss such a personal and intimate matter, preface your discussion by verbally reaffirming your love and commitment to
each other. Say to each other something like, "I
love you—and our relationship is more important to me than our current concerns."

> *Key point:* Before you work on discussing and
> improving the sexual aspect of your rela-
> tionship, make sure you are both rested,
> relaxed, and in somewhat of a good mood.

> *Common trap:* Treating a sexual difficulty as if
> it were more important than the relation-
> ship itself, even though you know it is not.
> *Solution:* Compare how much of your time
> is spent thinking about and discussing
> your sexual concerns, as compared to other
> aspects of your relationship. Strive to
> spend the vast majority of your time work-
> ing on enjoying or improving the overall
> relationship, as opposed to focusing on just
> one part of it.

6. Do you tend to think that your identity or self-
worth is associated with sexual activity or performance? If so, please see Central Principle 5:
"Self-Worth," page 58.

7. Do you tend to think your happiness or personal
sense of security is associated with sexual activity or performance? If so, please see Central
Principle 6: "Personal Security," page 74.

Barrier 5

Missing Ingredient(s) in the Relationship

COMMON INDICATORS

Thoughts: "Something is missing in our relationship. If things were going better sexually,
everything else would be fine."

Feelings: Tension, hurt, numbness, etc.

Actions: Overinvolvement in one area of life (sex,
work, children, recreation, hobbies, etc.).

GENERAL INFORMATION

If an essential ingredient is missing in a marriage, the
delicate balance between psychological, physiological,
emotional, and spiritual factors necessary for sexual intimacy will be disrupted. Sexual difficulties can be a
healthy warning signal that something in the relationship requires attention and correction before satisfactory
intimacy can be resumed or obtained.

Interesting Note: Approximately 90% of sexual
problems clear up spontaneously when missing
personal or marital ingredients are taken care of.

STEPS TO REMOVING THE BARRIER

1. Make a list of the satisfactory aspects of your
marriage.

2. Examine your list to see if you are missing anything you would consider absolutely essential for a good marriage. Examples: Respect, kindness, commitment, communication, responsibility, hygiene, problem solving skills.

   Caution: Having some sexual difficulty does not necessarily mean an essential ingredient is missing. If you do not find any missing ingredients, see other barriers.

3. If you do find a missing ingredient, ask yourself some important questions. Do you really consider that ingredient to be an absolute necessity for you to have a good marriage or are you willing to learn to get along without it?

   Key point: If you consider a particular ingredient an essential requirement for your marriage, it must be corrected before sexual intimacy can be mutually satisfactory.

4. Utilize sexual difficulty as a healthy warning signal reminding you to examine yourself and the relationship, looking for essential areas in which to make corrections or improvements.

   Caution: Ongoing sexual activity or disagreements about sexual matters can unintentionally prevent the identification and correction of missing marital ingredients.

5. If, for some reason, you feel obligated to make love, consider whether you can honestly and sincerely do so as long as that important ingredient is missing.

Ask yourself:

"How long can you continue to make love out of obligation and still respect yourself and your spouse?"

6. Decide that adding the essential missing ingredient is more basic and important to your marriage than the current sexual concerns. Agree with your spouse that both of you will initially work harder on providing the missing ingredient than on trying to correct the sexual difficulties.

7. If, however, he insists on continuing sexual activity without acknowledging and working on providing the missing ingredient(s), you have an important decision to make. Do you wish to participate in frosting the cake while a basic essential ingredient is missing?

8. If you decide to temporarily postpone sexual activities until progress is made in working toward providing the missing ingredient(s), write a brief note to your spouse. Include:

   • What you appreciate about your spouse.

   • Your concern about the missing ingredient(s).

   • Your specific hopes for a better relationship.

   • What actions you are currently going to take.

   Caution: If your intent is genuinely respectful and constructive, as opposed to manipulative, you can proceed, even if your spouse does not understand at first. However, if your intent is to postpone sex to get your spouse to make some changes, you are out of line. Your intent, as much as your actions, determines whether you are being respectful and constructive or whether you are being manipulative.

9. Frequently reassure your spouse of your love and of your desire to strengthen and build the relationship. Repeatedly let him know you expect the sexual difficulties will be resolved after taking care of the missing ingredient(s).

   Reason: When one person makes a change in sexual behavior, it is very easy for the other person to interpret the change as being manipulative, even if it is not, or to misunderstand the message and think he is not worthwhile or lovable.

10. If, however, after a few weeks you and your spouse are not working together or making progress, consider seeking professional help. (See Appendix, "How To Select A Therapist.")

Basing Your Security or Happiness On Your Spouse

COMMON INDICATORS

Thoughts: "How can I feel secure when he spends more time with work, church, recreation, etc., than he does with me?" "I cannot be happy unless he . . ."

Feelings: Insecure, easily upset.

Actions: Walking on eggs so as not to displease him. Nagging.

Please see Barrier 8: "Basing Your Security or Happiness on Your Companion," page 103.

Too Busy, Too Tired, or Just Not Interested

COMMON INDICATORS

Thoughts: "I'm too tired. Not tonight."

Feelings: Pressure, resentment, guilt, numbness.

Actions: Avoiding or surrendering.

GENERAL INFORMATION

Just as you cannot fully enjoy a fine dinner when you are tired, rushed, or in conflict with yourself or your spouse, intimacy is no different. If your life is out of balance, it is unlikely you will be able to fully enjoy intimacy.

For sex to be truly intimate and meaningful, it not only takes a great amount of love and attention outside the bedroom, but a great amount of emotional energy and work in the bedroom. Ironically, some people put more preparation into going out to dinner than into making love. If you do not have enough energy to participate in intimacy, let alone enjoy it, it is unreasonable to force it.

Key point: Most sexual difficulties are prevented or corrected outside of the bedroom.

STEPS TO REMOVING THE BARRIER

1. Take time to go to the doctor and get a complete

physical if you have not had one in the last year—just to be on the safe side.

2. Review how you spent your time during the last week. Take a piece of paper and make seven columns, one for each day of the week. On the left side of the paper write various times of the day, beginning with the earliest time you might arise, to the latest time you would go to sleep (not just go to bed). Fill in the columns with your activities during the last week.

3. Evaluate how well you balanced your life between work, marital, family, and personal activities. Are you getting enough rest, exercise, and nutrition?

   Caution: If your life is out-of-balance in any of these areas, intimacy is not likely to be satisfactory except perhaps in a brief physical sense.

4. Consider how much time you spent last week with your spouse in a pleasant, relaxed, enjoyable, and uplifting manner, independent of any sexual activity. How much time did you spend just talking in a friendly, unrushed manner?

   Key point: Unless you both agree that you have shared some quality time together, intimacy is not likely to be very intimate.

5. Discuss what can be done to increase the quality time you share together. Ideas: have a weekly or monthly business-like lunch, have a daily or weekly telephone conversation, take a regular walk, go out on a weekly date, write each other a weekly letter.

Result: Just spending time together, regardless of what you do, provides an opportunity to revitalize the relationship, relieve stress, prevent or solve problems, and create an environment where love can be more fully and satisfactorily expressed.

6. Discuss what usually occurs during the hour preceding lovemaking. Consider whether those activities are relaxing, refreshing, romantic, etc.

Key point: Although you can rush through fast-food restaurants, making love is more like enjoying dessert after a fine meal.

7. Discuss the preparations and conditions necessary for you and your spouse to enjoy a fine dinner and dessert together. *Reason:* Many of the principles and practices associated with a successful meal are similar to those necessary for successful intimacy. Notice the importance of not being rushed, overly stressed, or more concerned with the meal than with each other. Consider how you treat each other before, during, and after the meal.

Key point: Notice how you give the entire meal your attention and enjoyment, rather than focusing mainly on the dessert.

8. Plan a special dinner out together and see what you can learn about intimacy.

9. If you do not seem to be finding sufficient opportunities to make love, consider providing regular periods of time where you can privately enjoy being together, whether or not you become physically intimate.

Example: Go to bed an hour early a few times a week to talk, read, or just be together—without any pressure to make love. *Result:* By providing the opportunity to be intimate, without any pressure or demand to do so, you will increase the likelihood of mutually desirable and satisfactory intimacy.

10. Observe how you convey your love to each other immediately after being physically intimate. Do you hug, kiss, hold hands, quietly talk, say something loving, etc.? If you almost immediately roll over and go to sleep, consider what message you may inadvertently be sending your spouse.

SUCCESS STORY

Although Brian and Mary Lou loved each other very much, the sexual aspect of their marriage was deteriorating. For quite some time, Mary Lou's interest in making love had been decreasing. She seemed to be more and more going through the motions without the emotions.

Brian was a good man, but there were a few things that really bothered Mary Lou. It seemed like the only time he wanted to be physically close was when he wanted sex. Mary Lou hesitated to tell me the other thing that bothered her because it seemed so trivial. I reassured her it is often the accumulation of the small things that slowly erode intimacy in a marriage. Mary Lou finally told me that Brian sometimes had bad breath.

Even though there were many times she wanted to say, "No," to having sex or ask him to use a mouthwash, she did not because she believed his needs were more important than her feelings. When she did muster up the courage to say "No," Brian, though not abusive, was obviously upset. For quite awhile, Brian did not realize anything was wrong, but, when he did become aware, he suggested Mary Lou see a counselor. He was certain he did not have any "sexual problems."

SEEKING SOLUTIONS

Mary Lou came alone to my office, as do about half of those with marital concerns, seeking help for what she was afraid was her problem. As Mary Lou explained their situation, I did not try to figure out who was to blame or who had the "problem," rather I wanted to determine what resources were available to create a solution. It did not take long to determine each of them had important responsibilities for obtaining a solution. Mary Lou quickly caught on to my message that we were going to shift from her problem-oriented approach, which asked a lot of "whys?" and tended to point fingers, to a solution-oriented approach, which looked to each spouse as having experiences, ideas, and skills that will contribute to a solution. The result was a lot of relief and hope.

REDISCOVERING HER RIGHTS

When I asked Mary Lou about her rights relative to intimacy, she seemed a little confused because she thought mainly of her husband's rights and her duties. We discussed her rights in other aspects of her life, and she realized her thinking was clear and she generally stood up for what she believed. "Do you have the right to say 'Yes' or 'No' to intimacy?" I asked. She was unclear of where the line was between her rights and his needs. I explained, "Unless you have the right and the skill to say 'No,' you are not truly free to say 'Yes.'" Nor was she free to fully enjoy intimacy. Intellectually she knew she had such rights, but she was afraid that by exercising her rights she might deny Brian of something he needed.

I explained that sexual desire is a powerful passion and appetite, rather than a "need" like food or water. Whether Brian knew it or not, he was quite capable of rationally postponing sexual satisfaction, if necessary, in order to make a few important personal and relationship adjustments. Then they would be able to more fully enjoy their relationship, as well as the frosting on the cake.

Mary Lou was still hesitant about saying "No" and upsetting Brian until she realized he only had the *tendency* to become upset—he did not have to become upset. It was up to him. Even if he initially was upset, he was quite capable of later understanding that she still loved him and was simply doing a few things differently so they could have a better marriage.

> *Caution:* If Mary Lou said, "No" nicely and her intent was manipulative, her actions would be disrespectful and counterproductive. She assured me she was not trying to use sex as leverage to make Brian change. She just wanted to have the right to say "Yes" or "No," depending on how she felt at the time.

SETTING MINIMUM STANDARDS

Mary Lou's next step was to see that she had a basic right to determine for herself the conditions under which she was willing to be intimate. At first she thought I was suggesting she try to dictate to Brian how he had to behave—that she was going to try to make him do what she wanted. I reassured Mary Lou that any such intent on my part or her part would be disrespectful, manipulative, and simply wrong.

I asked, "If Brian wanted to make love on the front lawn, would you do it?"

"Certainly not," she immediately replied. She was able to respond so quickly because of her personal standards or prerequisites for intimacy. Her requirement had nothing to do with trying to dictate or control Brian; it was simply her intention to exercise her right to be intimate under conditions she found acceptable.

One of her homework assignments was to make a list of her minimum standards or requirements for intimacy.

Mary Lou asked if she could put something as simple as clean breath on her list. I assured her that was certainly her choice, and besides, it seemed to be a reasonable requirement.

SHARING HER INTENTIONS

I asked Mary Lou to return home and gently explain to Brian what we talked about and how she believed they would soon be able to have more enjoyable intimacy now that she better understood that they both had certain rights. I asked her to invite Brian to write up his own list of minimum standards for intimacy before she shared hers with him.

Even though her explanations to Brian were kind and her intentions were respectful, he still misinterpreted her independence as being manipulative and threatening. He was hurt and angry. He thought because they loved each other, making love should just occur naturally without any demands placed on him.

I asked Mary Lou to write a loving letter explaining (1) her appreciation for Brian; (2) her concerns about their deteriorating love life, and (3) her thoughts of what they could do about it. She explained she wanted to have more times when they talked, shared feelings, held hands, hugged, or kissed without any pressure or expectation to have sex. She added that a little bit of breath freshener or mouthwash would also be helpful. Mary Lou closed the letter by reassuring Brian of her love for him and that she had absolutely no desire to withhold something from him that he enjoyed, nor any desire to force him to change. She too wanted things to be closer and better for both of them.

RESPONDING TO THE CHANGES

After a few weeks on an emotional roller coaster ride, Brian came in to see me, as most reluctant companions eventually do. He had seen Mary Lou become stronger and realized, too, that she loved him very much, even though she was indicating a few things needed to be changed. He admitted he was not very comfortable with being close except in bed, but he wanted to learn. As Brian learned to express affection in nonsexual ways, they both became happier as they drew closer together. The irony for this couple was that Brian was so happy and satisfied with their newfound closeness, there were even a few times when he was the one who said, "No."

Summary

A brief summary of key principles and actions, necessary to resolve unsatisfactory intimacy is provided.

KEY PRINCIPLES

- ❑ Sex is easy. Intimacy, though, is more involved.

- ❑ The central feature of intimacy is not emotional or physical; it is commitment.

- ❑ When intimacy is fully developed or restored, sexual difficulties tend to disappear.

- ❑ Emotional discomfort, whether fear or dissatisfaction, is usually a healthy indicator suggesting that something with you, your spouse, and your relationship would benefit from some attention and improvement.

- ❑ Although problems with intimacy can affect feelings of self-worth, the fact of your inherent, God-given worth remains unchanged.

- ❑ Sexual intimacy is like the frosting on a well-baked cake, with all the essential ingredients in it. If an essential ingredient of the cake is missing, sexual intimacy is unlikely to be satisfying.

KEY ACTIONS

❏ If your marriage is not more important to you than any other relationship, activity or possession (except your relationship with the Lord), reevaluate your priorities.

❏ Rather than attempting to control feelings, including sexual desire, work on controlling your thoughts and actions, thereby affecting how you feel.

❏ Respectfully discuss with your spouse the meaning that each of you attaches to sexual intimacy.

❏ Be careful not to base your self-esteem or personal security on sexual activity or the lack thereof.

❏ Make a list of the satisfactory aspects of your marriage. See if anything you consider absolutely essential is missing. If so, examine yourself, and if appropriate, discuss it with your spouse.

❏ Make sure you are getting sufficient food, exercise, and sleep—otherwise, you will not have enough energy for intimacy.

❏ Only participate in sexual intimacy when both of you feel good about it.

Reminder: *Be sure to review the Central Principles section. Identify the principle(s) not effectively being utilized. Then take the appropriate steps to apply the principle(s).*

ANXIETY ATTACKS

OVERVIEW

The time we live in has been aptly referred to as the Age of Anxiety. Therefore, not surprisingly, people experience varying degrees of anxiety throughout their lives. By the time a person reaches the teenage years, dreams of living a peaceful and anxiety-free life have already begun. Unfortunately, despite the ideals of youth, no one escapes anxiety regardless of their achievements. Wealth, beauty, position, power, athletic success—none of these are any protection against anxiety. Some people, however, experience so much anxiety that it interferes with living happily.

RIDING THE WAVES OF ANXIETY

Rather than learning to safely and effectively ride the waves of anxiety, many people inadvertently increase anxiety by battling their anxious feelings. They wage a war and try to force anxiety away. Millions attempt to control or escape the unpleasantness of anxiety through T.V., caffeine, alcohol, nicotine, drugs, or sex. Others fight anxiety in their minds. They develop an artificial calmness or aloofness, giving an illusion of security and stability. People who appear unusually calm on the surface are frequently just the opposite inside, although, sometimes their self-induced numbness is so successful they do not realize the extent of their internal turmoil. Some people mentally fight anxiety by becoming preoccupied with work, finances, their health, or any number of things.

COMMON REACTIONS TO INTENSE ANXIETY

Many people experience an extreme form of anxiety that hits like a lightning bolt out of a clear blue sky. This type of anxiety is referred to as an "anxiety" or "panic" attack because of the sudden onset of extreme physical symptoms. The symptoms can be so intense they seem to signal an impending disaster—even death. Sometimes breathing becomes so rapid, a person gasps for air while his heart pounds with an increasing velocity. Other symptoms include sudden perspiration, uncontrollable trembling, numbness, dizziness, or inability to swallow.

What can be shocking is the sudden occurrence of the anxiety or panic attack—often without warning. Someone who has experienced constant anxiety or nervousness may never have such an anxiety attack, whereas a person who never had problems with anxiety may develop a serious problem without any apparent reason. Extreme anxiety can also occur without any association to a particular event or situation. For instance, a person may simply wake up in the middle of the night gasping for air.

Extreme anxiety, however, is frequently associated with a particular circumstance. The initial "attack" may occur sometime following a medical problem or in association with a particular situation that never caused any intense reaction in the past. Some people, for instance, may never have experienced difficulty shopping alone, riding an elevator, crossing a bridge, flying, or eating in public when they unexpectedly have an "attack" in one of these situations. After that initial episode, it's understandable the person could be traumatized and become anxious about future participation in the activity he associates with the extreme anxiety.

For some people, just thinking about being alone might trigger extreme anxiety. Such individuals seek security in the company of other people, on the phone, or in person. Family and friends become a type of security blanket to the individual who is convinced that his life depends on having someone nearby at all times.

LOGIC BEHIND ANXIETY

Some of my most intelligent, imaginative, and successful clients have experienced anxiety attacks. They cannot figure out why they would be experiencing such "ridiculous, irrational reactions." The intensity with which they analyze and fight their symptoms is commendable but often makes matters worse.

There is good news about anxiety though: for those willing to look and learn, it provides valuable information about how a person is operating, just as an automobile's instruments provide information on how it is operating. Anxiety is a warning signal similar to a trouble light on the dash of an automobile. It is not to be ignored or controlled. Learning to catch those signals early and utilizing the invaluable, though often unpleasant information, allows people to troubleshoot and make quick corrections before problems develop.

Without correct information and proper direction, many people suffer needless pain and anxiety. As a person comes to understand the logic behind anxiety, he can learn to quickly catch subtle warning signals far in advance of the "attack," thereby preventing the more serious symptoms.

One of the biggest hurdles in understanding anxiety attacks is the difficulty in distinguishing the myths from the facts. The following section will help dispel some of the myths.

Myths and Facts

Whether you are reading this book seeking help for yourself or are involved with teaching or helping others, your success will be directly related to the ability to sort myths from facts concerning anxiety attacks. Following are ten of the more common myths and their corresponding facts.

1. *Myth:* Anxiety attacks are caused by medical problems, such as heart disease.

   Fact: Anxiety attacks are rarely caused by medical problems, although the way a person responds to medical problems can produce various degrees of anxiety.

2. *Myth:* Anxiety attacks can cause a person to pass out while driving.

   Fact: If a person is driving an automobile when symptoms begin, he will naturally, and safely, tend to pull over to the side of the road before the symptoms become too severe.

3. *Myth:* Anxiety attacks can kill.

   Fact: Even though a person may feel his heart is going to explode or he is not going to be able to breathe, it takes much more than anxiety to kill a person. Just ask any emergency room physician who has seen hundreds of healthy people who had sincerely believed they were going to die from an anxiety attack, leave the hospital well and intact.

4. *Myth:* If a person feels he is going to die, then he will.

   Fact: Feelings, no matter how sincere or powerful, do not change the medical fact a person is not going to die from an anxiety attack.

5. *Myth:* Experiencing extreme anxiety means a person has lost control of himself.

Fact: Even though a person may not be controlling his response to feeling anxious as well as he might, he is still controlling his thoughts and actions.

6. *Myth:* Certain situations cause anxiety attacks.

Fact: Although anxiety may occur in association with a particular event or situation, the situation itself does not cause an anxiety attack. Rather, the manner in which a person responds to a situation or to feelings of anxiety, determines whether the anxiety symptoms subside or intensify.

7. *Myth:* Anxiety attacks can be avoided by avoiding certain situations.

Fact: Avoiding situations actually reinforces the irrational belief that situations control anxious feelings rather than recognizing that the individual controls his anxious feelings. The result is a greater feeling of helplessness and anxiety.

8. *Myth:* When anxiety symptoms first occur, the best thing to do is try to make them go away.

Fact: Trying to force unpleasant feelings to go away is like trying to put a grease fire out with water—it just makes things worse. It is better to acknowledge and accept the fact of "feeling anxious," while beginning or continuing to do something constructive, until the emotional waves pass.

9. *Myth:* To eliminate anxiety attacks, it is necessary to know how and why they got started.

Fact: Learning to respond to feelings of anxiety in ways that minimize it, through rational thinking and behavior, is more important than discovering how or why the attacks began.

10. *Myth:* Anxiety attacks will be eliminated when a person achieves emotional security.

Fact: Emotional security is at best a fleeting feeling, and at worst, an illusion futilely sought after like the proverbial pot of gold at the end of the rainbow. Real security has more to do with how well you manage yourself than on how you feel.

Before elaborating on how to minimize and eventually eliminate anxiety attacks, it will be beneficial to gain a better understanding of how an anxiety attack develops.

ANATOMY OF ANXIETY ATTACKS

To better understand the cause of an anxiety attack, consider how the immune systems works. It is designed to produce cells or antibodies, which fight to ward off enemy invaders to the body (viruses, foreign tissues, etc.). In an allergic reaction, however, the immune system goes awry. It turns against and attacks the very body it was designed to protect, thereby producing symptoms such as runny nose, itchy eyes, or asthma.

Emotional or physical pain, like the immune system, is intended to play a warning or protective role in a person's life. An anxiety attack, however, begins as your mind and body relentlessly attack in an attempt to eliminate its own emotional warning signals. Attacking anxiety—rather than responding to anxiety as a natural warning signal suggesting some personal action—can bring about an anxiety attack. Although not all anxiety attacks begin in the same way, most people go through steps similar to the following:

1. A person first experiences some mildly unpleasant physical sensations such as dizziness, fatigue, warmth, rapid heart rate, or difficulty breathing.

2. He consciously or unconsciously attempts to control bodily sensations he cannot directly or immediately control.

3. The physical symptoms not only persist but become more intense.

4. He imagines what might happen if he is not able to get his body under control. As a result, the initially mild physical sensations become increasingly severe.

5. He doubts his body's natural ability to recover without his own conscious intervention.

6. He tries to make his body immediately calm down but fails.

7. He begins to conclude that he has lost control of himself and something awful is about to happen. *Result:* Panic! The physical symptoms now mimic those of an impending heart attack.

8. He goes through some extreme, often irrational actions, in order to find relief. He may refuse to leave his house, insist on having someone to talk to every minute, or repeatedly seek medical help despite being told nothing is medically wrong.

9. He believes that whatever he was doing when his symptoms finally subsided, caused him to feel better. *Fact:* His symptoms would have eventually subsided, in their own natural way and time, no matter what he did or where he did it.

10. After the symptoms subside, he has difficulty learning from his experience. Instead, he becomes inordinately introspective and dependent on others and may limit or avoid activities.

Understanding the anatomy of an anxiety attack will help you to identify and remove the barriers to overcoming anxiety attacks.

Barriers to Overcoming
Anxiety Attacks

There are seven common barriers that interfere with successfully dealing with anxiety attacks:

Barrier 1: Self-defeating goals.

Barrier 2: Fighting to control anxiety.

Barrier 3: Difficulty distinguishing feelings from facts

Barrier 4: Basing personal security on feeling calm.

Barrier 5: Vivid imagination.

Barrier 6: Feeling unsure how to prevent or respond to an anxiety attack.

Barrier 7: Trying too hard to help others.

Self-defeating Goals

COMMON INDICATORS

Thoughts: "I've got to find a way to get rid of these feelings."

Feelings: Anxiety about feeling anxious.

Actions: Avoiding situations perceived as anxiety producers or staying in "safe" situations.

GENERAL INFORMATION

When you are having difficulty accomplishing a goal, it is natural to question whether you are trying hard enough or whether something is wrong with you. Sometimes, however, it is neither. The goal itself can be the problem. Unrealistically high goals, for example, can cause anxiety.

When your main goal is to *feel* better ("Feeling" goal) rather than to *do* better, you usually end up feeling worse. When your main goal is to *do* better ("Doing" goal), hoping in the long run if not sooner, to *feel* better, you usually end up doing and feeling better.

STEPS TO REMOVING THE BARRIER

1. Watch for these common self-defeating goals:

   • Trying to be perfect right now. Perfection is not possible during the few short years we live on this earth.

- Trying to control anxiety. Anxiety is viewed as the enemy rather than as a healthy warning signal that something in your life can be improved.

- Trying to avoid situations believed to be responsible for undesirable emotions such as shopping centers, freeways, bridges, or elevators. *This* shifts responsibility for solutions away from yourself to the environment, which cannot always be controlled.

- Trying to control people or situations you cannot really control. By doing this you are mentally hitting your head against the wall.

- Trying to find relief through another person's presence. This shifts responsibility for solutions away from yourself to others. Promotes unhealthy dependency.

2. Think of several occasions when you overcame feeling anxious.

    Key point: Every time you have ridden the wave of anxiety to its crest, you have also ridden it down to the point of feeling comfortable again. How did you do it? What were your goals? This results in increased awareness of what has worked for you in the past.

3. Notice how your goals that resulted in feeling better had little, if anything, to do with directly *trying* to feel better. They usually focused on thinking or doing something, rather than on trying to feel better.

Examples of "Doing" goals:

Situation: Your heart is loudly pounding prior to giving a speech.

Doing Goal: Concentrate on notes and look at only a few friendly faces in the audience.

Situation: You break out in a cold sweat in the grocery store.

Doing Goal: Remind yourself you are still physically healthy and you only feel as though you are having a heart attack. Focus on finding the items on the shopping list and completing the purchase.

Situation: You have difficulty breathing while driving.

Doing Goal: Safely pull over and listen to soothing music until the emotional volcano finishes erupting and passes. Resume driving to destination.

4. **Look for opportunities when you are not extremely upset to choose between a "Feeling" goal or a "Doing" goal** in order to more readily comprehend their differences. When you pursue a "Feeling" goal, notice what is different from when you pursue a "Doing" goal.

   Example: No matter how hard Lorraine tried to feel relaxed going shopping, she failed. In fact, the harder she tried to feel comfortable, the more uncomfortable she felt. Rather than trying so hard to feel comfortable, she switched to a "Doing" goal of simply getting the shopping done. With her new goal she succeeded just about every time. Although the anxiety did not immediately disappear, at least she felt good about accomplishing her main goal—doing the shopping.

5. Begin each day with a written list of "Doing" goals—goals you are going to pursue, regardless of how you feel.

   Key Point: As you put less energy into trying to control or eliminate certain feelings, you will have more energy to do whatever you wish.

Fighting to Control Anxiety

COMMON INDICATORS

Thoughts: "I've got to get myself under control." "I must make myself relax or else . . ."

Feelings: Anxious or frightened about not being able to control feelings; loss of confidence.

Actions: Running from a situation or reaching out to be rescued, or both.

GENERAL INFORMATION

Sometimes when you are extremely anxious, you may find yourself making a common mistake—attempting to futilely control, fight, or eliminate the stream of emotion. As a result a dam is created that blocks the natural flow of emotion, thereby causing unpleasant feelings of anxiety to grow in magnitude and intensity. Rather than simply acknowledging the unpleasant feelings of anxiety—and finding a way to better manage yourself or your circumstances—you end up with compounded or dammed feelings. Now you have two problems: the original anxiety and dammed anxiety.

Example: Occasionally Boyd felt a tightness in his chest. Although several visits to the doctor failed to find any medical problems, he began to worry that the tightness might lead to not being able to breathe. He decided to fight the tight feeling himself by breathing more rapidly. Without realizing it, his attempt to control anxiety symptoms by over breathing caused a second problem—the lowering of carbon dioxide in the blood and subsequent feelings of numbness, tingling of the hands, and dizziness. The harder he tried to breathe, the worse he felt. This vicious cycle is often referred to as hyperventilation.

Rather than fight the symptoms, I suggested he apply the common cure for hyperventilation: place a paper bag over your head and face, loosely covering your nose and mouth; breathe normally for five to fifteen minutes; take a small breath approximately once every five seconds; and breathe through your diaphragm instead of your chest. Your stomach will move in and out instead of your rib cage. Boyd did this and with more carbon dioxide in his body—and no more fighting of the initial feelings by over-breathing—he gradually began to feel better.

Rather than fighting to control anxiety—which generally causes more anxiety—it is much better, at first, to learn to control the way you respond to the emotional symptoms. As a result, *there are* no more anxiety attacks.

Fortunately, the common symptoms of an anxiety attack (rapid heart beat, rapid breathing, numbness, dizziness, and difficulty breathing), naturally tend to subside when left alone to run their course. Although little can be done to immediately make the storm go away, fighting the feelings only serves to prolong and intensify them.

STEPS TO REMOVING THE BARRIER

1. Think of a time you felt nervous when, instead of trying to control the feelings, you focused your attention on controlling something else.

Example: Most people accept feeling nervous before an athletic or musical performance as normal and try to weather, rather than fight, the discomfort as best they can. As soon as the performance begins, they focus on what they are doing as opposed to how they are feeling, and the nervousness naturally subsides and disappears.

2. Remind yourself of the body's natural, God-given ability to heal and calm itself down as long as there is no artificial interference. Think of times you trusted your body to successfully take care of itself with little or no help.

Examples:

- When you had a cold or virus, you knew it was just a matter of time before you would be feeling better again. *Reason:* You trusted your immune system to do its job, even though you may not have fully understood how it worked.

- After a vigorous physical workout, you were confident your rapid heart rate, perspiration, and fatigue would subside in a reasonable amount of time. *Reason:* You had faith in your body's natural ability to calm down.

- After eating, you knew the food would be digested and properly used by the body without any effort on your part. *Reason:* Again, simple faith in your body.

3. Every day, notice at least three times when your body naturally and automatically corrects itself. As you do this you will begin to regain some of

the faith and confidence you lost in your body's ability to survive.

4. Think of times you felt extremely anxious. Remember what happened when you tried to make yourself feel calm. A good example of this is trying to get sweaty palms dry before an important meeting—the harder you tried, the worse it got.

5. Think of a time you experienced something similar to an anxiety attack but responded by just reassuring yourself and letting it run its course.

   Example: Recently I was jolted out of my sleep by an earthquake and thought the house was going to collapse and that I would die. I was scared to death. Shaking uncontrollably I could hear my heart pounding. It took about an hour before my body relaxed enough to go back to sleep. Not until the second or third day did I feel completely normal.

6. Think of an anxiety attack as an automobile engine overheating. As the steam is pouring out, you control your response by waiting for the engine to cool off before attempting to do anything. Even after the steam subsides, it takes additional time before the engine is cool enough to work on. If you tried to control the steam or make the engine cool off prematurely by throwing cold water on it, you could burn yourself or damage the engine.

7. Instead of fighting your emotional steam, decide to observe the intensity with interest and a rational realization that it will eventually subside.

Rather than trying to control how much steam comes out of your emotional engine, control the reassuring thoughts you run through your mind.

Repeat to yourself:

"I will allow my body to blow off steam and cool off. Then I will take preventive or corrective action."

---

8. While waiting for the anxiety symptoms to subside, do something simple and meaningful despite the intense feelings—lie down and let the emotional earthquake run its course, take a walk, listen to some music, vacuum the living room, or read a book.

Key Point: If you do any of these with the intent to force the wave of internal motion to subside, you will unwittingly cause it to escalate.

Difficulty Distinguishing Feelings from Facts

COMMON INDICATORS

Thoughts: "I am a feeling person. Going against my feelings would be dishonest. So when I am afraid to go outside, I do not leave my house."

Feelings: Volatile and conflicting.

Actions: Debating with self, disregarding important facts.

GENERAL INFORMATION

Just as instruments in an automobile provide essential information for safe driving, feelings provide necessary information for making wise, sensitive, and rational decisions. For example, if your head—and the objective facts—say you are reasonably healthy and safe while your heart is pounding rapidly, it is generally better to rely on your head. Important decisions are best made with 90% head and 10% heart.

Key point: No matter how strong feelings may be, they cannot change the facts.

STEPS TO REMOVING THE BARRIER

1. Make more objective and sensitive decisions, by taking the following actions:

- Take several 3x5 cards, write down the two important principles below:

> *Important decisions are best made with 90% head and 10% heart.*
>
> *Feelings do not change facts.*

- Place the cards where you can see them at least a dozen times a day (on your refrigerator, T.V., bathroom mirror, or visor of your automobile).

- Whenever you find your head and heart in conflict, let the conflict act as a trigger to remind you to repeat to yourself the words on the cards.

> Say to yourself:
>
> *"Important decisions are best made with 90% head and 10% heart. Feelings don't change facts."*

- To increase your understanding of these two principles, discuss them with others

2. Make a list of past, present, or potential situations where your head and heart are not in total agreement. *Note:* The fewer such situations, the happier and more at peace you will be.

Examples:

- The *fact* that you have a healthy body is not changed because you *feel* like you are going to die.

- The *fact* that you have inherent worth is not changed because you *feel* worthless.

- The *fact* that someone has had too much to drink is not changed because he *feels* he can drive safely.

- The *fact* that you have certain skills is not changed because you *feel* inadequate.

3. For each situation you wish to resolve in which your head and heart are in conflict, take a piece of paper and draw a vertical line down the center. On one side of the line write down all the pertinent facts that come to mind.

   On the other side of the line write down your feelings. If there are any feelings not supported by facts, place a big question mark by those feelings. For example, your heart is medically healthy yet sometimes you feel you are having a heart attack; or you have a college degree yet you feel unintelligent. As a result you are now in a better position to objectively and sensitively think about your situation.

   For addition information, please see Central Principle 3: "Feelings versus Facts," page 40.

Basing Personal Security on Feeling Calm

COMMON INDICATORS

Thoughts: "I can't stand to feel upset." "I can't do anything until I feel better." "I need to feel better before I act."

Feelings: Insecure.

Actions: Trying to appear calmer than you feel. Avoiding situations where you feel uncomfortable.

GENERAL INFORMATION

Traveling through this life, you may sometimes experience more anxiety and insecurity than you prefer. If, however, you attempt to find an anxiety-free way through life—in a futile attempt to feel secure—ironically you will experience even more anxiety and insecurity. *Reason*: You avoid learning and participating in events that provide for the development of greater security. Since eMOTION is constantly in MOTION, basing any sense of security on naturally unstable feelings is in and of itself insecure.

STEPS TO REMOVING THE BARRIER

1. Think of times you felt insecure but in fact had every reason to feel quite secure. *Example*: Tad

frequently felt anxious and insecure during graduate school, even though he ended up receiving straight A's.

2. Remind yourself of the importance of doing something constructive regardless of how you feel.

> Ask yourself:
>
> *"If I'm going to feel uncomfortable for awhile, would I rather feel uncomfortable and get something done, or would I rather feel uncomfortable and get nothing done?"*

3. Practice doing constructive things, even though you do not initially feel comfortable doing them. *Result*: The more you do so, the less uncomfortable you will feel, and if you continue to feel uncomfortable for awhile, at least you have accomplished something constructive.

4. Look for things you can do to bring greater happiness and security, even though they may not make you feel good immediately. For example, exercise regularly; eat moderately; get sufficient rest; involve yourself in church, civic, academic, or professional activities; read a good book; visit a friend; etc.

For additional information, please see Central Principle 6: "Personal Security," page 74.

Vivid Imagination

COMMON INDICATORS

Thoughts: "I can see it now . . ."

Feelings: Frequently feeling an intense eruption of emotion.

Actions: Daydreaming, dwelling on upsetting events, putting yourself in other people's circumstances.

GENERAL INFORMATION

Imagination has many facets. Most everyone enjoys gazing up at beautiful clouds, visualizing vivid, imaginative shapes and scenes. Imagination can also create frightening monsters out of shadows on a bedroom wall. Imagination can picture the happy reunion of a loved one coming home for the evening . . . or burning to death in a fiery automobile accident. How you use your imagination is completely up to you. You create your own movies. One client remarked, "I didn't realize the pictures I view in my mind are multiple choice." If you have developed the habit of using imagination in a negative way, it will take time and practice to get it under control.

STEPS TO REMOVING THE BARRIER

1. Think of times you have used imagination in healthy, constructive ways such as relaxing;

visualizing a goal; enjoying a book, movie, or music. Also, be aware of times you currently use your imagination in a healthy way.

Warning: Do not attempt to eliminate the possibility of negative imagination by unnaturally forcing positive thinking.

2. When you find yourself visualizing an unpleasant event (whether real or imagined), consider whether or not your thinking is constructive.

> Say to yourself:
>
> *"Important decisions are best made with 90% head and 10% heart. Feelings don't change facts."*

Result: By frequently asking the above question, your mind will automatically become more skilled in effectively managing the use of imagination.

3. If you wish to calmly think about an unpleasant event, think about it as if you were hearing it reported on the radio or on T.V. Say to yourself, "Three people were killed in the automobile accident, PERIOD. And I refuse to create or dwell on any mental pictures of it." Then get busy and focus your attention on something constructive even though some unpleasant emotions may linger for awhile.

4. If you tend to become overly anxious about possible disasters in your life or the lives of your loved ones, occasionally say "Yes" to picturing the event. Imagine not only surviving the event,

but more importantly, picture what you will be doing as you effectively get on with your life.

Example: I found myself feeling anxious about the unlikely possibility something horrible might happen to our son. Late one night, as I watched him peacefully sleeping, I let myself imagine the worst had happened. Just the thought of losing him caused my eyes to well up with tears. But I did not end the picture there. I allowed myself to picture what I would be doing a few weeks after his death. I saw myself being with my wife, working, going to church, even jogging. I was sad, but I could see life going on. As a result, I am less inclined to imagine the worst coming to pass, because I am confident I could survive and life would go on.

5. Review the sources and types of information (positive or negative) that come into your mind each day. Especially examine your habits associated with T.V., radio, newspapers, books, and magazines. Also, think about the information shared in your daily conversations.

6. Minimize, or in some cases eliminate, the upsetting or frightening information you take into your mind.

7. When you think or talk about a situation, notice the words you are using. Are you using imaginative, Hollywood words (often upsetting) or plain, objective, and factual words?

Examples:

Hollywood: My daredevil husband drives like he is in the Indianapolis 500.

Plain fact: My husband often drives 10 to 15 miles per hour over the speed limit.

Hollywood: My heart is going to explode. It is beating like a drummer in a rock band.

Plain fact: My heart is beating a lot faster than usual.

Hollywood: I can't breathe. I think I'm going to die.

Plain fact: I'm having difficulty breathing.

8. Notice how you feel when you use Hollywood words. Practice substituting plain, objective, and factual words.

Note: Once the physical sensations of anxiety are triggered, however, changing words will not cause the body to immediately relax. The longer you were thinking the upsetting thoughts, the longer it will take to feel calm again. As you develop habits of using fewer emotionally charged words, you will feel less anxious in the future.

Unsure How to Prevent or Respond to an Anxiety Attack

COMMON INDICATORS

Thoughts: "How can I prevent anxiety attacks?"
"What do I do when anxiety attacks
occur?"

Feelings: Worried, discouraged.

Actions: Trying one technique after another.

GENERAL INFORMATION

Just as in sailing a ship one does certain things *before* problems occur to help prevent their occurrence, *during* the occurrence of problems to make corrections before things get worse, and *after* problems have occurred to learn from the mistake and minimize or prevent future problems, the same is true for dealing with the waves of anxiety. As you increase your knowledge and skills in the three previously mentioned areas, you will be better able to minimize and eventually eliminate anxiety attacks.

STEPS TO REMOVING THE BARRIER

The steps for removing this barrier are divided into three sections: *Before* an anxiety attack, *during* an anxiety attack, and *after* an anxiety attack.

BEFORE AN ANXIETY ATTACK

1. Involve yourself in a well-balanced variety of constructive activities such as work, school, family, church, social activities, physical exercise, music, or service. If your life is out of balance in just one area, you will have difficulty making any lasting improvements. Regular aerobic exercise such as walking, jogging, bicycling, or swimming are especially helpful.

2. Develop a healthy mental diet just as you do a physical diet. Feed your mind constructive, uplifting food. Avoid upsetting thoughts as you avoid unhealthy food.

   Key point: What you feed your mind determines what kind of mind you will have.

   Example: People who read wholesome and uplifting material daily are more likely to ride out waves of anxiety without becoming upset than people who read about upsetting things. At the very least, they will be able to overcome anxiety attacks more quickly.

3. Recall some of the anxiety-producing thoughts you tend to think about. Then make a list of those thoughts. Equate your list to identifying the weeds beginning to invade your garden.

4. Seek to be aware of thoughts preceding or triggering an anxiety attack before it occurs and immediately divert your thoughts and attention to something more constructive.

DURING AN ANXIETY ATTACK

1. Determine the degree of anxiety you are experiencing by rating it on a scale of one to ten, with ten being the most intense anxiety ever experienced. Say to yourself, for example, "My body is at a six or a seven."

   Caution: Do not cause additional anxiety by saying "I *am* at a six or a seven." *Reason:* It is easier to manage your body than your entire being.

2. Acknowledge and accept the degree of anxiety you are experiencing, without trying to force the intensity to go down—especially if the intense anxiety hits suddenly like an earthquake.

   > Say to yourself:
   >
   > *"Before I can feel better, I need to accept the fact my body is at a nine, and I am going to feel crummy for a little while."*

   Caution: Resist the temptation to analyze why you are having an attack while you are experiencing it. *Reason:* Unless asking why leads to an action-oriented solution, it will just make you feel worse—especially if you do not come up with a reasonable answer.

3. Reassure yourself you will indeed survive, no matter how badly you currently feel.

> Say to yourself:
>
> *"Though my feelings seem to be saying I'm dying, my head says otherwise; and when in doubt I choose to believe my head."*

4. Despite how you feel, do something construc-tive—even if it is something small.

   Caution: Do not just think about how you feel. Do something.

AFTER AN ATTACK

1. Even after your thoughts and activity are back within bounds, be patient with the way you feel. The length of time it takes your body to relax after extreme anxiety is about ten times as long as the time you were feeling anxious. The ripples in a pond continue long after the rock that caused them is resting on the bottom.

2. Reassure yourself you can learn a great deal from feeling upset, as long as you resist the temptation to ignore your feelings or condemn yourself for having them in the first place.

3. Think about what you can learn from getting upset so you can do something better next time.

> Ask yourself:
>
> *"What could I have done to prevent myself from getting so upset?"*
>
> *"Once upset, what could I have done to minimize the intensity and duration of the feelings?"*

4. Instead of just trying to learn from your mistakes, think of some of the times you started to get upset, but instead of dwelling on it, got yourself involved with something else. Think about how you did it. Ask yourself what was different during those times.

Key point: Too often people spend more time dwelling on their mistakes rather than on analyzing and learning from their successes, especially if the successes appear to be an accident or an exception to the norm.

You may wish to study the accompanying chart on the following page to gain a clearer overview of the three different areas of dealing with anxiety attacks.

How to Respond to an Anxiety Attack

BEFORE

GOAL: Prevent or minimize anxiety attacks

METHOD:
1. Involve yourself in constructive activity, designed to keep your life in balance.
2. Develop a healthy mental diet.
3. Identify and avoid anxiety producing thoughts.

RESULT:

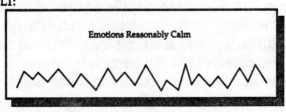

Emotions Reasonably Calm

DURING

GOAL: Ride out the wave and get through the storm.

METHOD:
1. Monitor the intensity of the anxiety on a scale of 1 to 10.
2. Acknowledge and accept the existence of the anxiety without trying to fight or control it.
3. Reassure yourself that you will survive.
4. Do something constructive despite how you feel.

RESULT:

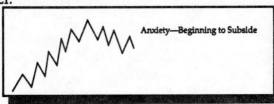

Anxiety—Beginning to Subside

AFTER

GOAL:
1. Learn to respond to future anxiety attacks in a more rational way.
2. Learn to prevent future anxiety attacks.

METHOD:
1. Be patient with any lingering, undesirable feelings.
2. Reassure yourself that you can learn a great deal from your mistakes.
3. Do not condemn yourself for having an anxiety attack.
4. Determine at least one thing you can specifically do to improve yourself.

RESULT:

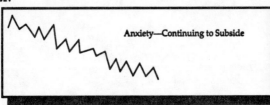

Anxiety—Continuing to Subside

Trying Too Hard to Help Others

COMMON INDICATORS

Thoughts: "I've got to do something to help him."
"I can't stand to see him so unhappy."

Feelings: Sympathy, frustration, resentment.

Actions: Unnaturally altering normal routines, repeatedly talking about the same things, etc.

Please see DEPRESSION, Barrier 10: "Trying Too Hard to Help Others," page 204.

SUCCESS STORY

Amy was a talented lady in her early thirties. She was active with family, part-time work, church, community service, and a regular program of jogging. Her physician said she was in perfect health—yet she was having horrible physical symptoms.

Amy explained to me how shocked she was when suddenly, while she was shopping, her heart started racing wildly, her breathing became difficult, and her body began perspiring. She went to the local emergency clinic on three separate occasions thinking she was having a heart attack. The doctor called her symptoms an "anxiety attack" and suggested she simply go home, try to relax, and perhaps see a therapist.

She was frustrated with so many well meaning people treating her trauma lightly. "Just go home and relax," they would tell her. She was already trying so hard to relax she was becoming anxious about not being able to do so. It is understandable how frightening it can be when you feel like your body is about to explode. Feeling like she was going to die did not change the medical fact that Amy was an extremely healthy lady. I assured her I had never heard of anyone dying from an anxiety attack even though the intensity of the symptoms would seem to suggest otherwise.

Although Amy understood what I was saying, she did not feel any better. She just wanted to know how to get rid of the extreme anxiety and make sure she never felt that way again. "There is a logical explanation behind every anxiety attack," I explained. Amy began to understand the anatomy of an anxiety attack. She then began to imagine how, shortly down the road, but not right away, she would have the necessary skills to become free from future anxiety attacks.

TRUSTING THE BODY'S NATURAL ABILITIES

First, it was necessary for Amy to once again trust her body's ability to recover from an emotional wave. She would know when her trust was regained because she would stop trying to make her emotional symptoms go away prematurely. I told her about a chronic knocking sound in my automobile engine. I too wanted it to go away, but I knew the noise was an early warning signal telling me something needed correction. The mechanic was not as concerned with the noise as I was because he knew how to listen and diagnose the problem. He then explained what corrections were necessary. Like the mechanic, I showed Amy how to listen to her anxiety and use it to help identify the things she could do to significantly improve her life and reduce anxiety.

REGAINING SELF-RELIANCE

A short time later, Amy bravely made an important decision. She decided if she started to get extremely anxious again, she would resist the temptation to call the doctor, or even her family. That was a big step. She had often put her husband and mother in the awkward position of being her crutch when what she really needed was to regain confidence in herself to get through the problem on her own. Fortunately, she allowed me to speak with her husband and mother. I encouraged them to support her in overcoming anxiety attacks by lovingly being unavailable if she had another attack.

"What if she called in a panicky state saying she needed them?" they asked. I suggested three things. First, tell her they love her; second, state their faith in her ability to weather the storm on her own; and the third and most difficult, tell her they will talk to her later and politely hang up the phone.

After a couple of weeks Amy succeeded in not being so anxious about having an anxiety attack. She certainly did not want another one, but more importantly, she was gaining confidence in her ability to weather another anxiety storm if necessary.

A REASSURING EXPERIENCE

Amy recalled an experience she had as a teenager with many parallels and solutions to her current situation. A six-foot wave had knocked her down at the beach and held her under the water for what seemed an eternity. She remembered being unable to breathe and feeling like she was going to drown. Since there was no way she could successfully fight the wave, she wisely decided to let herself be tossed around like a shirt in a washing machine, while she offered a short prayer pleading for help to be able to hold on till the wave passed. She went with it, rather than fighting it. Amy reassured herself that thousands of people survive after being pulled under by waves like this one. It seemed to last forever until, somehow, she finally found herself safely washed ashore.

Later on, she shared her frightening experience with others who had gone through similar situations and reflected on what she had learned. She found she had gone out too far from shore and had not been paying attention to the waves building in intensity. Amy realized how to avoid getting into difficulty again. I suggested whenever she thought about having an anxiety attack, or if she was actually having one, to reflect on her beach experience.

After a couple of more weeks, Amy felt she fully understood the logic behind her anxiety attacks and what was necessary to avoid getting in trouble again.

REBUILDING A BALANCED LIFE

At this point we looked at other areas in her life that were out of balance. She had a tendency to get overinvolved with people and activities. She decided to learn to say "No" to some of the many people and activities demanding her attention and time, in order to take better care of herself. At first she felt a little selfish and guilty but soon found ways to reasonably determine how much she could handle. Amy was well on the road to overcoming her problem.

I had not seen Amy for several months when she called me with a triumphant tone in her voice. She related how tempted she was to call me a few weeks earlier after becoming quite anxious about a burglary in her neighborhood while she was home alone. But she did not call. Her anxiety was understandably intense, but she said it did not get to the point of an anxiety attack. Amy had learned to manage herself and her circumstances. She saw the wave this time and rode it to shore.

A summary of the key principles and actions Amy and many others have utilized in overcoming anxiety attacks is provided next.

Summary

Following is a brief summary of key principles and actions necessary to minimize anxiety and eventually eliminate anxiety attacks.

KEY PRINCIPLES

☐ Anxiety is a warning signal similar to a trouble light on the dash of an automobile. Anxiety is intended to be observed and utilized, rather than controlled, in order to prevent or correct problems.

☐ Trying to force unpleasant feelings to go away is like trying to put a grease fire out with water— it just makes things worse.

☐ Although anxiety may occur in association with a particular event or situation, the situation itself does not cause an anxiety attack. Rather the manner in which a person responds to the situation or to feelings of anxiety, determines whether the anxiety symptoms subside or intensify.

☐ The body has a natural ability to calm itself after experiencing a wave of anxiety.

☐ Feelings do not change facts. For example, the fact of having a healthy body is not changed because of feeling otherwise.

❑ Personal security depends more on how you manage yourself and your circumstances than on how secure you feel.

❑ Important decisions are best made with 90% head and 10% heart.

KEY ACTIONS

❑ Avoid self-defeating goals designed to control anxiety ("Feeling" goals). Instead, set "Doing" goals, focusing on improving what you do with your thoughts and actions. In doing this, you will gain better control over yourself and eventually feel less anxious.

❑ Seek ways to minimize anxiety and eliminate anxiety attacks by trusting your body's natural ability to calm itself down rather than by trying to fight or control the anxious feelings.

❑ Use your imagination in positive ways. If it is desirable to think about unpleasant things on occasion, describe the event in your mind with objective words, rather than with vivid pictures.

❑ Develop strategies for dealing with anxiety attacks in three different areas: before, during, and after their occurrence.

Reminder: *Be sure to review the Central Principles section. Identify the principle(s) not effectively being utilized. Then take the appropriate steps to apply the principle(s).*

Appendix

HOW TO SELECT A THERAPIST

If you were going to hire a tutor—or any employee—you would would naturally tend to interview a variety of possible candidates, questioning each thoroughly in order to find the right person. You would want to find out as much about the individual's technical skills as you would about their character. You would also want someone with whom you feel comfortable. Often, however, people spend little if any time shopping around for a qualified therapist. They mistakenly assume if one has an advanced degree and a license, he or she is qualified.

When you are in the market to hire a therapist, it is highly important to find someone who meets your specific personal requirements for the job. Whereas most people know what they want in a tutor, the qualities comprising an effective therapist may not be as clear. Some of the characteristics I would look for in a therapist are suggested below:

CHARACTERISTICS OF AN EFFECTIVE THERAPIST

1. Willingly and competently answers any of your questions, especially relative to his or her objectives and method of treatment.

2. Answers your questions in a simple and practical manner.

3. Speaks to you as an equal in a down-to-earth, easy to understand manner.

4. Focuses on goals and results rather than theories of how or why the problems began.

5. Focuses on the present, as opposed to the past.

6. *Teaches* you how to change habits of thinking and behavior rather than just analyzing how or why they came about.

7. Often provides you with assignments or exercises to work on between visits.

8. Is moderate and reasonable in speech and appearance.

9. Understands and respects your moral and religious values.

10. Displays confidence in your ability to learn how to solve your problems and in his or her ability to teach you.

11. Has experience in successfully dealing with your specific type of problem.

12. Generally expects counseling to be successfully completed in a few weeks or months, not years.

FINDING AN EFFECTIVE THERAPIST

In order to find a therapist qualified to assist you, I would encourage you to interview at least three therapists before you select one—unless you already know one who meets your needs. With each interview you do, you will gain more knowledge about the variety of therapists and therapies available; you will then become a better informed and wiser consumer. A brief telephone interview is generally sufficient. If a therapist will not take five to ten minutes on the phone to answer your questions, you can probably rule him or her out right away. Once you select a therapist, your first visit will provide you with additional opportunities to ask questions and to assess his or her qualifications. If you are not satisfied with the therapist you selected, find another one.

POSSIBLE QUESTIONS TO ASK

1. What is your approach to therapy?

2. After providing the therapist with a brief statement about your problem, ask, "How would you go about helping me solve it?"

3. How much experience and success have you had in treating my type of problem?

4. How long is it apt to take to solve my problem? (Of course, an exact answer is not possible, but a reasonable estimate can be expected.)

5. What are your goals when you provide therapy?

6. How much emphasis do you place on the past versus the present?

7. What kind of things would you expect me to be doing between our appointments?

8. Would you be supportive of me in my religious beliefs?

9. Last of all, ask for his or her opinion about any issue that is important to you that could be controversial. For example: whether or not it is worth trying to save a dying marriage; whether or not divorce is a viable option; whether or not extramarital affairs, abortion, homosexuality are acceptable, etc.

Remember: When you hire a therapist, he or she is your employee—you are the boss.

Index of Examples

INDEX

NOTES